Who Do Men Say That I AM?

VOLUME ONE

KEN STEWART D.MIN.

ISBN: 979-8-9926864-0-1 (Paperback)
ISBN: 979-8-9926864-1-8 (eBook)
Copyright © 2025 by Kenneth E. Stewart, D. Min.

All rights reserved under International Copyright Law. No portion of this book may be reproduced in any form without written permission from the publisher or author except as permitted by U.S. copyright law.

This publication is designed to provide accurate and authoritative information in regard to the subject matter covered. It is sold with the understanding that neither the author nor the publisher is engaged in rendering legal, investment, accounting, or other professional services. While the publisher and author have used their best efforts in preparing this book, they make no representations or warranties with respect to the accuracy or completeness of the contents of this book and specifically disclaim any implied warranties of merchantability or fitness for a particular purpose. No warranty may be created or extended by sales representatives or written sales materials. Neither the publisher nor the author shall be liable for any loss of profit or any other commercial damages, including but not limited to special, incidental, consequential, personal, or other damages.

First edition 2025

Unless otherwise noted, all Scriptures marked KJV are taken from the KING JAMES VERSION (KJV): KING JAMES VERSION, public domain.

Scriptures marked AMP are taken from the AMPLIFIED BIBLE (AMP): Scripture taken from the AMPLIFIED® BIBLE, Copyright © 1954, 1958, 1962, 1964, 1965, 1987 by the Lockman Foundation Used by Permission. (www.Lockman.org)

Scripture marked AMPC are taken from the AMPLIFIED® BIBLE, CLASSIC EDITION, (AMPC) Copyright© 1954, 1958, 1962, 1964, 1965, 1987 by the Lockman Foundation Used by Permission. (www.Lockman.org)

Scriptures marked ESV are taken from THE HOLY BIBLE, ENGLISH STANDARD VERSION (ESV): Scriptures taken from THE HOLY BIBLE, ENGLISH STANDARD VERSION ® Copyright© 2001 by Crossway, a publishing ministry of Good News Publishers. Used by permission.

Scriptures marked EXB are taken from THE EXPANDED BIBLE (The Expanded Bible) (EXB): Scripture taken from THE EXPANDED BIBLE. Copyright© 2011 by Thomas Nelson, Inc. Used by permission. All rights reserved.

Scripture quotations marked (MEV) are taken from THE HOLY BIBLE, MODERN ENGLISH VERSION. Copyright© 2014 by Military Bible Association. Published and distributed by Charisma House.

Scriptures marked NIV are taken from the NEW INTERNATIONAL VERSION (NIV): Scripture taken from THE HOLY BIBLE, NEW INTERNATIONAL VERSION ®. Copyright© 973, 1978, 1984, 2011 by Biblica, Inc.™. Used by permission of Zondervan

Scriptures marked NLT are taken from the HOLY BIBLE, NEW LIVING TRANSLATION (NLT): Scriptures taken from the HOLY BIBLE, NEW LIVING TRANSLATION, Copyright© 1996, 2004, 2007 by Tyndale House Foundation. Used by permission of Tyndale House Publishers, Inc., Carol Stream, Illinois 60188. All rights reserved. Used by permission.

Scriptures marked NKJV are taken from the NEW KING JAMES VERSION (NKJV): Scripture taken from the NEW KING JAMES VERSION®. Copyright© 1982 by Thomas Nelson, Inc. Used by permission. All rights reserved.

Scripture marked KJ21 are taken from The Holy Bible, 21st Century King James Version (KJ21®), Copyright © 1994, Deuel Enterprises, Inc., Gary, SD 57237, and used by permission.

Contents

Preface i
Introduction 1
Chapter 1 His Astonishing Three Years 9
Chapter 2 His Place in The Trinity 23
Chapter 3 His Role as The Son 35
Chapter 4 His Unity with His Father 49
Chapter 5 His Words - His Works 57
Chapter 6 His Determination 73
Chapter 7 His Challenge to Us 79
Chapter 8 His Imitators 87
Chapter 9 His Family 99
Chapter 10 His Close Friends 113
Chapter 11 His Disciples 137
Chapter 12 His Other Six Choices 173
Chapter 13 His Betrayer 189
Chapter 14 My Conclusions 201
Epilogue 209
Notes 213
About the Author 219

Preface

This manuscript began as a study of the most powerful and effective ministry in history. Without question, this is the ministry of Jesus. I wanted to know how Jesus did the wonderful things that are recorded in the Gospels. My desire was to present more than the typical recitation of His sermons and miracles. And I don't mean to imply that these are insignificant. They aren't! I just had something else in mind that I wanted to share with my readers.

My original goal was to help you confront the issue of Jesus being a man, yet a man who performed miracles. It does not seem that most Christians see Jesus that way. We think of Him being born as a human baby. But when we think of Jesus as an adult, our opinion of Him seems to change. Suddenly, Jesus becomes God. I thought I could clarify many of these things with a clear and simple discussion of His ministry.

However, as I wrote the manuscript, I realized the direction of my thoughts had changed. It became clear to me that to understand the ministry of Jesus, it was necessary to have a better understanding of who Jesus was and is. I realized that this is where we have often missed the clues Jesus gave us. We must never separate who He was from what He did. This assumes that we know who Jesus was. Do we?

The vital importance of this is found in the fact that Jesus never changes. Therefore, this is a book about who Jesus is. In the typical sense, this book is not about His ministry. It is about Him. Who was He? Who is He? I think we have a pretty good understanding of who Jesus was as a baby. But what about now? There seems to be things about His ministry, and especially His miracles, that alter our view of Him.

When a ministry functions as God designed, there is no logical or meaningful way to separate the man or woman from the ministry. Yet, they are not the same. They are two significant parts of the whole. Who the man is determines what the ministry becomes. Who the woman is determines what the ministry becomes. This explains why so many ministries have ended in disappointment and disgrace. Typically, a ministry does not change the man or woman. They change the ministry.

It is this tension between the person and the ministry and miracles that drew me into this path of discovery. At the outset, I thought the best way to describe the ministry of Jesus was to talk about Him instead of writing about what He did. This was the direction of the Holy Spirit. I was on the right track but did not realize it at first. I soon discovered there is so much to know about the person we call Jesus that it needed to be a book by itself. Then, it turned into two books. And my, what a series this has become. It is all there in the Bible if we will just take the time to see it.

I knew that if I had the chance to ask my readers to describe the ministry of Jesus, they would talk about what He did. While I am extremely interested in how Jesus did the things He accomplished, I am much more interested in why He did them. It seems clear to me that the reason behind the actions Jesus took tells us much more about Him than the events themselves. The numerous facets of this book explain the "why." As you read these pages, think of it in that way.

In a conversation with His disciples, Jesus asked them the question that is the title of this book and the next volume as well. It seems strange that Jesus would be asking questions of mere men. Yet He did. He wanted to know what they thought. He wanted to know what they believed.

He wants to know what you think and believe. You may think He already knows. Even if He does, He wants to hear you say it. What is your opinion of the Son of man? Does your opinion of the Son of man influence your opinion of the Son of God? It certainly should. I have answered these questions for myself. If the contents of this manuscript do not answer those questions for you, perhaps they will steer you in the direction of your own answers.

One word that will appear many times in both volumes is the word relationship. That word may have a more significant meaning for you by the time you finish reading these books. This book will tell you much about Jesus, but it will not create a relationship with Him. The relationship we need only comes from spending time with Jesus. Knowing the right things about Jesus will cause you to want to spend time with Him. That is the real purpose of both of these books. So, talk to Him. He is listening. Talk to Him often.

Some people call that prayer, and I have no argument with that. I simply choose to think of it more as two friends having a conversation. Jesus is the best and the closest friend I have. What about you? Is He your friend? Are you His friend?

Over the many months it has taken me to form these thoughts and put them into the words found in this book, I have spent a lot of time talking to my friend. I wanted to be sure He approved of what I was writing about Him.

No doubt you already know a great deal about Jesus. Don't allow that to cause you to think you can't benefit from what I have written. I have known Jesus all of my life, and in some ways, these two volumes are a reflection of that lifelong relationship. Yet, I constantly discover things I did not know about who He is.

My great desire for you is for you to have this same experience. That is why I wrote this book and the one that follows it. Perhaps, at some time in the future there will be a book about the things Jesus did. We will see. But even if that does not happen, I will certainly not ever regret the many hours I spent assembling these vignettes to present the clearest picture I could of the Lord of my life.

Introduction

Authoring a book about Jesus is a daunting task. Except for the abiding help of the Holy Spirit, I would never have embraced such an assignment. I don't know if this is logical to you, but to me, it almost seems intrusive. By that, I mean I hold Jesus in the highest esteem possible.

Among the many remarkable things about Jesus that must be considered is the shortness of His time on earth. Since we are only talking about approximately thirty-three years, it does not seem like it would be difficult to write about in some detail. However, we are not talking about just any ordinary person. This was the most perfect and most powerful man there has ever been. Jesus accomplished more in those thirty-three years than anyone else could achieve in thirty-three hundred years.

We can determine from the Scriptures that Jesus spent about thirty years getting prepared. That may seem odd to you, but it shouldn't. Proper preparation was essential. Jesus was a man on a mission. His was a job that did not allow for a wasted moment. To use a non-theological expression, once Jesus fully embraced His purpose, He hit the ground running and never looked back. John summed it all up like this in his Gospel writings.

> *There are also many other things which Jesus did. Were every one of them to be written, I suppose that*

> *not even the world itself could contain the books that would be written. Amen. (John 21:25 – MEV)*

That statement was written by someone who knew Jesus very well. It has convinced me that when Jesus said we would do greater works than He did, it is not likely that Jesus was referring to the volume of His work. Perhaps a group of people could match the volume of what Jesus did. But one person would never come close. I will do my best to describe how this balances out in the following pages. But for right now I am speaking of much more than the things He did. I am talking about who He was.

There are many facets to this subject. I think we can get so caught up in the thrill of the miracles and the people being healed that we forget what made these things possible. There was a deep and abiding relationship between Jesus and His Father. How anyone could read the pages of the Bible and not see this relationship unfolding before their eyes is something that has always baffled me. I have worked hard in what I have written to make this revelation inescapable.

We would do well to begin with this relationship between a Heavenly Father and an earthly Son. What caused Jesus to be the man that He was? Yes, He was, and He is a man. Just making that statement confuses a lot of people. They don't think of Jesus as a man. After all, He was, and He is, the Son of God. Jesus was, and He still is, both, but becoming a man was essential to His becoming the person both God and man needed on this earth.

Introduction

The estrangement that had existed because of the fall of man in the Garden of Eden could only be resolved by a sinless man willing to give His life to save us from sin and make us righteous. Sin had brought death, and that death had passed upon all men. The Bible is clear about this.

Being both human and the Son of God was certainly much more of a challenge for Jesus than it will ever be for us. We may wrestle with it in our minds, but it was an everyday issue for Jesus. I can think of no better example than what happened to Jesus after He spoke in the Synagogue in His hometown. Here is a summary of what transpired.

Jesus read a passage from the Isaiah scroll. Among other marvelous things, this passage speaks about someone who is anointed to open blind eyes and set captive people free. It talks about the Spirit of the Lord being on this person, and they can do all sorts of miraculous works.

After Jesus read these words from the scroll, He rolled it up, handed it back to the attendant, and sat down. So far, everything had been going smoothly. But the Bible says that Jesus began to speak to the crowd in the Synagogue, and this is what He said.

> *"Today this Scripture is fulfilled in your hearing."*
> *So all bore witness to Him and marveled at the gracious words which proceeded out of His mouth. And they said, "Is this not Joseph's son?" He said to them, "You will surely say this proverb to Me,*

> *'Physician, heal yourself! Whatever we have heard done in Capernaum, do also here in Your country.'* Then He said, *"Assuredly, I say to you, no prophet is accepted in his own country. But I tell you truly, many widows were in Israel in the days of Elijah when the heaven was shut up three years and six months, and there was a great famine throughout all the land; but to none of them was Elijah sent except to Zarephath, in the region of Sidon, to a woman who was a widow. And many lepers were in Israel in the time of Elisha the prophet, and none of them was cleansed except Naaman the Syrian."* (Luke 4:21-27 – NKJV)

The people thought Jesus was very gracious until He began addressing their past failures. The people of Israel had repeatedly rejected the Prophets that God had sent to them. And now, they were about to do it again. Jesus knew it, so He decided to address it. The message Jesus often preached was a mixture of warnings and the plan of redemption. Accepting His message required change. And as it has always been, people just don't like to change. Many of them see no reason to change. Thus, provoking and providing a way for this change to transpire was the purpose of His preaching and teaching. We should be doing the same.

Many people still don't like that. They want the church to be a place where they are never challenged to make changes. The preacher should be nice. He should tell them how great they are. This does not seem to be working out very well.

Introduction

Jesus came to do much more than make people feel good about who they are. He came to change things. He came to die for our sins. He had a right to say the things He said.

If I go no further than this, you can see that Jesus was vastly different from much of what we see in many churches today. I had a pastor of a large church tell me that it was not his job to help the congregation apply the Word of God to their lives. He said he should just teach the Bible and let them figure out what to do with what he taught. After a few years, it became obvious those sheep never figured it out. Many of them had no idea how to live by what the Bible says.

Jesus sure did not do things that way. This passage is proof of it. So, already, we have learned some things about Jesus and His thought processes.

Jesus was very bold. He confronted the people about the way they were living. He was comfortable telling them what He was anointed to do. When they tried to put Him in His place by calling Him Joseph's son, He did not let that bother Him.

Only a few people have come close to doing the things Jesus did. Some have excelled in one area, such as their ability to teach, but failed in other areas, such as healing the sick. There is a reason for this. Most people seem to be afraid of what people think. They want to be liked, admired, and congratulated. This is much more important to them than speaking the truth in love.

Jesus knew they did not see Him as the Son of God. They only saw Him as a natural man. This was a problem, not so much for Jesus as for the people. In this context, Jesus said: *"Assuredly, I say to you, no prophet is accepted in his own country."* Not being accepted did not stop Jesus. If being rejected is something a person can't deal with, they will never do anything worthwhile. It just goes with the territory. The secret is learning how to deal with this in the right way.

Read the whole story about what happened in the Synagogue. It is amazing how quickly this situation turned from these people being pleased with the job Jesus had done to being so angry that they tried to kill Him. No one has ever tried to kill me. But this is not just about upsetting people.

How important is the truth? Does it matter that people do not like it when we confront them with their need to change? Or let's think about all of this the way Jesus did.

**Who do we want to please?
Is it our Father, or is it people?**

I will conclude my introduction with these remarks and questions. Jesus had the most difficult assignment any person has ever had, yet He was the most successful. Why?

What did Jesus do that was different? What were His secrets? Was Jesus only sharing things He had learned from other people, or did Jesus always have a fresh word from Heaven?

Introduction

How careful was Jesus about His close personal relationships? Now, that provides an interesting topic. It seems to be one that many Christians don't think about.

Did Jesus say and do all the things He said and did because He was the Son of God, or did He conduct His mission as a man? How can we tell? The answer to those questions may be the most important thing in this book.

Why does it seem like very smart people couldn't stump Jesus? How did He get so smart? Does this just mean Jesus was highly intelligent? Or could it be that as we learn more about who Jesus was, we will also learn more about the operation of the Holy Spirit and His gifts?

Jesus always had a lot of people around Him. Some of these people loved Him, and some of these people hated Him. One of the more interesting things about Jesus is that His family, other than Mary, did not seem to have much to do with His purpose for being here. Some of His cousins were involved, but most of His siblings were not. Thank God for those who caught on to what Jesus was about after He returned to Heaven.

A lot of the large and successful ministries of our day are comprised of a substantial number of family members. I am not saying this is wrong. It can be amazing to watch how they do things together. I am only observing that Jesus did not seem to have this. So, if your family does not support what you do in the ministry, don't let it bother you.

OK. That is a lot to talk about! And I have not even suggested that we discuss the signs, wonders, healings, and miracles. These have all received a lot of attention. I do think that attention is well deserved. It has certainly helped me through some tough times. But this book is about who Jesus was, not so much about what He did. So don't be too disappointed when you don't find those familiar stories in this book. That is not the purpose of this book. Look deeper!

Why do I consider who Jesus was to be so important that I would write two entire volumes about it? My answer is simple. Knowing who He "**was**" tells us everything we need to know about who He "**is**" today.

So, welcome to a fresh look at the person we call the Son of God and the Son of man.

Chapter 1
His Astonishing Three Years

Most of the things we hold dear about the time Jesus spent on this earth took place in about thirty-six months. We love the story of His birth and enjoy hearing about things that happened in His younger years, but what touches us so deeply is His earthly ministry, His death, and His resurrection. Of course, that abbreviated period of time Jesus spent on earth between the resurrection and the Ascension is especially intriguing. Those are the things that captivate our attention.

In my book on *The Holy Spirit In The Life Of Jesus*, I wrote extensively about the years before the ministry of Jesus began. None of that will be repeated here.

I also will not address His death and His resurrection. In fact, this will be the only mention of the time Jesus spent on earth after the crucifixion. Instead, I will address the title of this book. Just who was this man? I want you to grasp the significance of this question Jesus posed to His disciples. How much can we learn from what His disciples had learned?

The miracles and healings that occurred in the ministry of Jesus involved thousands of people. We are told in the Bible that they came to Jesus with all manner of sicknesses and diseases. Jesus touched them. If He was not touching them, then multitudes of them were touching Him and touching His clothes. What kind of man would do that? He never got sick. What kind of man never gets sick, especially when He is constantly around sick people? I want to know more about Him. Don't you?

There were countless miracles and signs and wonders. The Gospels are filled with the records of these tremendous and extraordinary events. What made it possible for this man we call Jesus to do these things? Many books have been written about the miracles and signs and wonders. But I want to know what was behind those things. How and why did they happen through this man? Who was He?

Jesus did so much in such an astonishingly brief time that it is absolutely amazing. He astounded, dumbfounded, thrilled, and even frightened some of those who saw these things occur. That much is clear from just reading the stories. This was, at times, the reaction of His disciples. But **how** did He do it? Why did He do it? I know why Jesus came to earth, but I want to understand why He was so willing to help people who did not know Him. Some of them even hated Him. Yet He kept on loving and giving.

Those words summarize the purpose and the content of this book. However, you should keep in mind as you read that the **who** encompasses the **how** and the **why** part of our subject. The real answer to **how** and **why** Jesus did things is knowing **who** He was. I know that may not be clear at this moment. But my plan is to make it truly clear.

I will let you in on a little secret. If we can't relate to **who** Jesus was, then we can't relate to **how** He did these great miracles, and we will never understand **why**. Jesus was the only begotten Son of God. I am not the only begotten Son of God. Yes, I am a child of God. But that does not make me a God. Thus, if the person **who** did these things was God, then it does not matter **how** He did them. At least, it does not matter personally because it is out of my reach.

If Jesus did all of these great things because He was God, this means I can't ever expect to do what He did. However, it means much more than that. It also means that what we have in our Bible is greatly distorted!

Believing that Jesus healed people and did miracles because He was God means that I have a lot of great stories to tell. However, it also means these wonderful events can never be repeated. At least humans can't repeat them. There are huge groups of people who look at the life and ministry of Jesus in this way. It is a colossal mistake!

Do you realize how much this undermines the current ministry of Jesus on this earth? Jesus taught and trained men to do what He did. Why would Jesus do that if they couldn't do it? Are we supposed to accept that three years of ministry was all God intended? Was that enough? How could this be the case when there are so many more people in need today than there were two thousand years ago? How beneficial is a history lesson to the person who is dying of cancer?

We will wrestle with these issues several times in the pages of this book. Can I explain it all? Probably not, but I don't need to. My goal is apologetic. However, I know my primary audience is comprised of those who already believe Jesus healed the sick, raised the dead, opened blind eyes, and cleansed the lepers. **Therefore, my ultimate focus is empowering believers to do what Jesus did.**

Let me say it again. The understanding of **how** Jesus healed the sick and performed miracles will not be found in the mechanics of how Jesus worked. The heart of the answer we are searching for lies in **who** Jesus was when He was doing these things. It is not a riddle. It is a remarkably simple but often overlooked Bible fact.

You may not think it is possible to do many of the things Jesus did, but I do. I have witnessed many of these things in my ministry, which motivates me to proceed. Yes, I have witnessed miracles. I have seen blind eyes open and have seen the lame walk. I have seen many people healed of cancer.

These things do happen.

Thinking about that makes me want to be more like Jesus. If **who** Jesus was had so much influence on what He did and how He did it, wouldn't the same be true for me? Wouldn't the same be true for you?

Jesus did the things I have mentioned, and we are supposed to be doing the same. Those words may surprise you if you don't know my basis for making such a statement. I can understand your surprise if you have been taught that these things have ceased. **They have not ceased!** So read very carefully with an open heart and an open mind. What you will find on these pages may turn your world right-side up. I am a recipient of one of these miracles. You can find the story of my miracle at www.drkenstewart.com.

I am telling you that the ministry of Jesus on this earth did not just last for a short three years. His physical presence on the earth ended, but not His ministry.

It was never difficult for Jesus to heal people and to perform miracles when the people believed in Him. As you continue reading this book, you will understand that this is a real problem today. Too many people, preachers and teachers included, just don't believe these same signs, wonders, and miracles can happen. Well, they can, and they do. I believe it, and I want you to believe it, too.

What happened in the ministry of Jesus when the people did not believe? It was catastrophic. Yet the way Jesus responded to this unbelief says a great deal about who He was. Unbelief is abundant today. I will give you a little hint. We should be dealing with this unbelief in the same way Jesus dealt with it. Unbelief can be conquered. But there is only one way to do it, and Jesus knew what that was. It takes a special kind of person to even want to do what Jesus did in the face of the unbelief which was specifically directed at Him. It would be amazing to see what would happen if more people started believing.

All of this will be discussed, and you will find many of the answers you have been searching for as I talk about how Jesus successfully met the needs of the people.

When Jesus was speaking in the Synagogue in His hometown, He announced what He had come to do for the people. His explanation was brilliant. Jesus used a prophecy from the Old Testament. It was one the people had heard about many times. However, they had never met someone who was willing to claim that this prophecy was about them. This claim about who He was almost got Him killed.

> *The Spirit of the Lord is upon me because he hath anointed me to preach the gospel to the poor; he hath sent me to heal the brokenhearted, to preach deliverance to the captives, and recovering of sight to the blind, to set at liberty them that are bruised, To preach the acceptable year of the Lord.*
> *(Luke 4:18-19)*

Jesus was clear that the areas of ministry spoken of by Isaiah were the things He had been doing and would continue to do. Yet, He never explained how He did them.

But what Jesus did on many occasions was explain who He was. Then, He followed this up with information about who was helping Him. Too many people have missed that part of what Jesus taught. Jesus was never alone until He hung on the cross.

From the crowd's reaction in the Synagogue that day, these people believed only God could do the things mentioned by the Prophet Isaiah. And they certainly did not believe that Jesus was God. But as my chapter titles indicate, these were all unique aspects of "His" ministry. They still are!

What if Jesus was human? What if He was just like us? What if that was a man who was opening blind eyes and cleansing lepers? Why would I ask such questions? I am asking them because of the intriguing answers they might provide. If Jesus could heal the sick because of some power or gift He had as a man, this opens the door to great possibilities. I am a man. Could it be that I might have access to this same power and this same gift?

That is a question that needs to be answered. Does the Bible provide this answer? I believe it does, or I would not have asked that question. The challenge is much greater than quoting a few Scriptures. A lot of people quote the Scriptures.

Let me restate the question. What if there is evidence that the power Jesus used is the same power we claim to have now? Is it the same power? If it is, then what is the problem? Is the real problem a matter of His gifts? Do we have those same gifts available to us today? I certainly think we have this same power and these same gifts available to us. But if I am right about this, then what are these gifts, and where do we get this power to do what Jesus did?

If I did not know that the answers to these questions are in the Bible, I might be like those who are satisfied to embrace the Holy Bible as a great history book. I might even convince myself that these were simply unfounded myths told by people who wanted to believe these things happened. I have met both kinds of people.

If you wonder why I would make such statements, it is because I spent six years in a very liberal seminary with professors who had accepted that way of thinking. These were brilliant men. Yet they were powerless to help people in serious need. They did not lack compassion and love. They simply had no power to set the captives free.

Compassion without power is almost useless.

These are not criticisms. These words express a part of what has motivated me to seek out the answers I am sharing with you. Much of the church world has preferred to leave this alone. I can't do that.

Numerous men and women before me have discovered enough about this topic to boldly act on what they knew. I am so glad they did. I knew some of them very well. I spent many hours with a few of them. This is another very personal reason for me to pursue this journey. I am discovering things I have never known, and I am compelled to put my findings in written form to help anyone who will receive them.

I do this with great anticipation of the results that may occur. Perhaps my words can be a catalyst to cause others to step out and **expect God** to do great things through their compassionate efforts. Now, there is an interesting concept.

Expect God? Yes!
Expect the ministry of Jesus to continue.

Fear is the first response many people feel at the very thought of attempting to heal the sick or work miracles. Those very words most often illicit an argument rather than ministry. The very idea of doing the things Jesus did seems to present us with the possibility of failure. At least, this is the most common reaction I have observed. This reminds me of something I read many years ago.

As I perused a friend's library, I picked out a book written by the late Oral Roberts. As I read the book, I came across a discussion Oral Roberts had with God. God had instructed Oral Roberts to begin praying for sick people. At that time, he had not done so. Once again, God had spoken to Oral and told him to begin praying for the sick.

Oral responded to God with this question. "But Lord, what if I fail?" The response that came back from God is one I will never forget. He said in his book that God responded.

"Oral, you have already failed because you have not done what I told you to do."

How many of us have already failed? We have not just failed to pray for the sick. We have not just failed to work miracles. We have not done our part to extend the ministry of Jesus beyond the three years He lived on this earth. Are you OK with that?

Your reaction could be that God has not told you to pray for the sick. May I remind you of these words that Jesus spoke many years ago?

> *And these signs shall follow them that believe; In my name shall they cast out devils; they shall speak with new tongues; They shall take up serpents; and if they drink any deadly thing, it shall not hurt them; they shall lay hands on the sick, and they shall recover. (Mark 16:17-18)*

If you are a believer these signs should be following you.

Oral Roberts was known for his ministry to the sick. He prayed for hundreds of thousands of sick people. This man had a profound effect on my life. Oral Roberts was a great man of God, but he certainly was not God. I am sure he would have told us that without hesitation. He was human, just like you and me. Yet, he must have discovered the power and the gifts that Jesus had. He not only discovered the power and these gifts, but he also used them.

It has brought immense joy to my life to see blind eyes opened and deaf ears unstopped. I have watched as those who were paralyzed got up and walked. I love to see the joy on the face of a person whose life has been changed by the power of God. I want to see more of this in the time I have remaining to minister. But I want to see this spread among those who are young, who have many years left to reach people in great need.

Let's examine those three astonishing years and discover what Jesus accomplished as a man. Of course, Jesus was not just a man. He was a man who had power and giftings that are also available to us. But then, we must also examine the things Jesus did because He was God. Jesus did things as a man, and He did other things because He was God. This entire issue must be resolved to correctly understand the Gospels. Not resolving this matter has created much confusion. Can we figure this out? I am convinced we can figure it out, and I am setting out to do it in this book.

The next question gets closer to home. Can I do the things Jesus did as a man? If so, how do I begin? Is there something that must change about me before I can do the things Jesus did? To what degree is "who I am" blocking me from the access I need to "how" Jesus accomplished His assignment?

Don't allow those questions to weigh so heavily on you that you decide not to pursue this. You are not limited to three years like Jesus was. You have the rest of your life to be used by God. What I am talking about is not something you are expected to do alone. You can't do these things without the aid of the Holy Spirit.

Thus, I am raising the issue of how we cooperate with the Holy Spirit. I will weave those answers into this exciting journey as we consider the many examples provided in the Gospels.

We will focus most of our attention on the four Gospels. However, I will incorporate many other Scriptures and use examples found in other places in the Bible. But my primary source will be the words written by Matthew, Mark, Luke, and John. They had first-hand knowledge of who Jesus was and what He did.

I make no apology for the fact that this book is written from a believer's perspective. We have these awesome, inspired sources available in the Bible. These men and women knew Jesus. They saw how He lived and watched what He did as they listened to what he said.

As we work through these pages together, if I briefly mention references that do not agree with what I have written, it will only be to contrast them with what the Bible says. I never know when I am writing who might at some point read my books.

Perhaps I can impact some of the doubt and unbelief that hangs like a dark cloud in the lives of so many. I certainly intend to do my best.

My in-depth study of "His Astonishing Three Years" of ministry has changed my life. More than ever before, I am a believer and not a doubter. I will have accomplished my mission if I can persuade you to believe.

On one occasion, when Jesus was teaching His disciples, He made these intriguing remarks about the lost.

> *But when he saw the multitudes, he was moved with compassion on them, because they fainted, and were scattered abroad, as sheep having no shepherd. Then saith he unto his disciples, The harvest truly is plenteous, but the laborers are few; Pray ye, therefore, the Lord of the harvest, that he will send forth laborers into his harvest. (Matthew 9:36-38)*

These words from Jesus are as relevant today as they were when Jesus first spoke them. Millions of people are lost and in need of guidance and support. They have no shepherd. The urgency of the mission is clear. We need more laborers in the harvest fields. I sincerely hope to inspire more men and women to join this mission, as I believe the time is now.

Chapter 2
His Place in The Trinity

Trinity is an unusual and intriguing word. In its purest form, it is unique to the Christian faith. Just the concept of the Trinity is fascinating. What makes it so interesting is that we have nothing on this planet to which we can compare this notion. We either believe in the Trinity, or we choose not to believe. There is no middle ground.

There are Christians who have been taught that there is a Trinity, and there are some who have been told this is a false doctrine. This divergence of opinions has caused a great deal of confusion and even animosity among different groups. The mere mention of the word Trinity can arouse many negative emotions among those who are adamantly against this teaching. Yet their efforts to explain what they believe about the Father, Son, and Holy Ghost are often very confusing. Only the word Trinity expresses the Biblical concepts we have of God. The Bible talks about three very distinct personalities. They have different functions. As impossible as it may seem, there is never any mention of conflicts between them.

Clearly, the concept of the Trinity is not a human invention. We have no details to express how this came to be and this is probably because we don't need to know. We simply need to believe in and appreciate what God has done.

I prefer to keep things as simple as possible. The Bible speaks of a Father, a Son, and the Holy Spirit. Why not accept that three Divine entities work together in perfect harmony?

Perhaps without even realizing it, when people remove this basic concept of Father, Son, and Holy Ghost from their theology, they change many other things they must believe. The Trinity is fundamental to understanding the rest of Scripture.

However, when I say that Trinity is an interesting word, I am considering my reason for including this chapter. My ultimate purpose is not to discuss the Trinity per se. What creates my current interest in the subject of the Trinity is that once Jesus was born in human flesh, Jesus was no longer just a deity. He is now both God and man. The only conclusion we can draw is shocking. Yet it is true. **There is now a human being involved in the Trinity.** Has that thought ever occurred to you? I have never heard anyone else mention it.

I will use this as a foundation for other things I have to say. However, it is possible or probable that someone will read this and have little or no understanding of what I mean by the word Trinity. So, I will include a very brief but straightforward explanation.

His Place in The Trinity

When the Apostle Peter was preaching at the home of Cornelius, he spoke briefly about the ministry of Jesus. I doubt that this group of people had ever heard of the Trinity. This would not have been common knowledge to those who only knew about the Old Covenant, much less to Gentiles. Thus, Peter did not use the word, Trinity. Peter was careful only to mention things that the Gentiles would have heard about. The word about Jesus had spread all over that part of the world. Peter made mention of this general knowledge about Jesus and by doing so, he confirmed it. Then, Peter went on to explain how Jesus could do the things that He did. In this explanation, we have an excellent reference to the Trinity. Perhaps it is best just to read his remarks.

> *The word which God sent unto the children of Israel, preaching peace by Jesus Christ: (he is Lord of all:) That word, I say, ye know, which was published throughout all Judaea, and began from Galilee, after the baptism which John preached; How God anointed Jesus of Nazareth with the Holy Ghost and with power: who went about doing good, and healing all that were oppressed of the devil; for God was with him. (Acts 10:36-38)*

John declared in one of his books that the purpose for which Jesus came to this earth was to destroy the works of the devil.[1] Luke (the man who authored the book of Acts) agreed with this conclusion on the purpose for which Jesus came to earth. But then Luke went even further, and by using the words from this message preached by Peter in the house of

Cornelius, he confirmed that Jesus fulfilled His purpose. Jesus did this with the anointing He had received from the Holy Ghost. Yes! Jesus relied on the anointing.

If Jesus needed the anointing of the Holy Ghost to fulfill His purpose, then we must also have the anointing of the Holy Ghost to fulfill our purpose.

There is much more to this message that Peter preached. In this message, we get a glimpse into how Jesus did the things He did. It was by the power of the Holy Spirit. Evidently, this is not enough information. Most Christians know about the Holy Spirit. Yet, they have never allowed His power to help them do anything.

The insight I am referring to can be found in this short phrase in the middle of Peter's statement.

How God anointed Jesus of Nazareth with the Holy Ghost and with power. (Acts 10:38)

In this statement, it is undeniable that three divine persons are mentioned in those few short words. They are the Father, the Son, and the Holy Ghost. Three completely different Greek words are used in this verse to indicate the three divine persons of the Godhead.

The Greek word translated as "God" is the word Theos.[2] This is the word the early Christians used to refer to the one true God. They found this necessary because of their society's polytheistic thinking. See the entry from *Vine's Expository Dictionary*.[3]

The Greek word translated as "Jesus" is the word iesous.[4] You may find the notes from the entry in *Vine's Expository Dictionary* to be interesting.

The Greek words translated Holy and Ghost are hagios[5] and pneuma.[6] These two words are defined as "a most holy thing" and "the third person of the triune God, the Holy Spirit, coequal, coeternal with the Father and the Son." Since it is not my purpose to provide a lesson in the Greek language, I will once again refer you to the same sources from which I have drawn other information. Those are the *Strong's Concordance* and *Vine's Expository Dictionary*.

The meaning of these four different Greek words provides an excellent understanding of the different members of the Godhead. Therefore, if we combine this understanding of the Greek words with the words spoken by the Apostle Peter, we can gain a better understanding of his statement.

How God anointed Jesus of Nazareth with the Holy Ghost and with power. (Acts 10:38)

God anointed **Jesus** with the power of the third person of the triune God. This is the same **Holy Spirit** who is coequal and coeternal with the Father and the Son. In this manner, all three members of the triune God were in some way working in concert to do the things Jesus did.

Is that a contradiction of what I have said previously? That could be your first reaction. I have said that Jesus did not do things because He was God. So, how is this not a contradiction? **The two members of the Godhead who are not human always worked with the one member of the Godhead who is human.** I encourage you to apply that information to the many stories in the Gospels about the things that Jesus did.

We should understand that the Father and the Holy Spirit want to work in concert with us just like they did with Jesus. **They are just as available to you and me as they were to Jesus.** I realize that may be shocking to some who read this. Nonetheless, it is certainly true. Otherwise, the Bible loses its personal meaning to us.

This may be hard to understand. However, what matters most is the answer to these questions: Is it possible for us to have the same anointing of the Holy Ghost that Jesus had? Yes! Can we expect to work in concert with the triune God the way Jesus did? Yes! Is it possible for a human being like you and me to do this? Yes! Or is this reserved only for members of the Godhead? No!

I have introduced this information about God into our discussion to point out that the Bible speaks of three distinctly different divine beings. This does not make our belief polytheistic[7]. We do not believe in three Gods. The phrase used in the last definition above states it very well. The Father, the Son, and The Holy Spirit are coequal and coeternal.

The Bible provides different word pictures for each of these divine beings. There are differences in their personalities, their responsibilities, and even in their actions. Yet, at the same time, they are always in complete harmony and agreement. They have one singular purpose and mission where mankind is concerned.

It is also interesting to consider that there was a time when God the Father was the person of the Godhead who had most of the contact with humans on this earth. That started with the time of creation and extended until the birth of Jesus. This covered several thousand years. Most of the information about this period of time is found in the Old Testament. I do think many people read the Old Testament, and the thoughts I have expressed never enter their minds.

With the birth of Jesus, the Son of God filled this same role on the earth until the time of His ascension back to Heaven. Then, after 40 days, the Holy Spirit assumed this role (only it became much more personal), and He still has this mission of interacting with man today.

My next statement is vital to understanding the remainder of this book. **In the Gospels, we see Jesus doing the things He did as an interaction between Jesus the man and the power of the Holy Spirit.**

Don't let it bother you if you don't understand that now. As you read this book, you will discover examples of what I have just said. I will explain and expound upon these concepts as I find them appropriate and helpful. While we see these three personages spoken of as separate entities, at the same time, we are given to understand they have one singular purpose. They always will. **The key to it all is how we interact with this singular purpose.**

Jesus did this perfectly. We probably will not do this as well as He did. This is why I am so focused on the fact that Jesus was both God and man. Jesus was a part of the Trinity before He was born in a manger. What intrigues me is that until the moment Jesus was born, thousands of years passed, and no human occupied a spot in the Trinity. Yet God's plan called for this change to occur. The beauty of it all is that it happened because of you and me.

This has a significant impact on what we believe. When I chose the title for this chapter, the fact that Jesus was just as human as we are was on my mind. I can find nothing in the Bible that hints that Jesus stopped being a part of the Trinity when He became a human being. That may hit you like a bomb, but it is true. We must filter this fact through the rest of what we believe about Jesus. We cannot resolve this in a matter of a few words. It will require both thought and revelation.

It is easy for me to embrace the concept that Jesus was co-equal with the Father and the Holy Spirit **before He was born as a baby and died as a man.** He was only God before those things happened. However, becoming a man changed Him forever. Now, Jesus is in Heaven, and He still has that new human body He had when He came out of the tomb. I am not trying to defend the title of this chapter. I am not even trying to explain it. I am trying to help you grasp what that means.

Some people will read these next statements and will not understand them, but I must write them for the sake of my allegiance to the Word of God. It is these words that come to mind.

For I am the LORD, I change not; therefore ye sons of Jacob are not consumed. (Malachi 3:6)

If I tell you that God has not changed and leave it there, you will think I have contradicted my previous paragraph. I wrote that when Jesus became a man, it changed Him. I do believe it changed Him forever. But how do we align my words with the words of this Scripture? That is precisely what I am attempting to do when I speak of Jesus being completely God and completely man.

Jesus is just as much God as He ever has been. Yet, from His birth until now and throughout all eternity, He will also be a man. The part of Jesus that is God or divine, if you prefer, did not change. An additional aspect of His very nature was added. Jesus also became a man. This had always been God's plan. Jesus must be both God and man for God not to have changed. If Jesus was not truly human, then God changed. That would not be Scripturally correct. **Therefore, it is not an acceptable idea.**

Because Jesus is so much like us He has done many things for us no other person could do. Jesus was not a sinner. The curse of death was not on Him. Jesus took our sin and died for us. But this means a member of the Godhead is a man. He is seated at the right hand of the Father. Yes, that is a man seated at the Father's right hand!

> *And you He made alive, who were dead in trespasses and sins, in which you once walked according to the course of this world, according to the prince of the power of the air, the spirit who now works in the sons of disobedience, among whom also we all once conducted ourselves in the lusts of our flesh, fulfilling the desires of the flesh and of the mind, and were by nature children of wrath, just as the others. But God, who is rich in mercy, because of His great love with which He loved us, even when we were dead in trespasses, made us alive together with Christ (by grace you have been saved), and raised us up together, and made us sit together in the heavenly places in Christ Jesus, that in the ages to come He might show the exceeding riches of His grace in His kindness toward us in Christ Jesus. For by grace you have been saved through faith, and that not of yourselves; it is the gift of God, not of works, lest anyone should boast.*
> *(Ephesians 2:1-9 – NKJV)*

It appears that, at least for some time, Jesus became less when He became a human being so that, ultimately, **we could**

become more. Exactly what it means to say Jesus became "less" is a challenging topic. This will be clearer when you read the chapter in Volume 2 about how Jesus prayed.

God has not changed. Jesus fulfilled His role in the plan of redemption. This required a man. It was necessary for this to be a perfect man. Only Jesus could do this.

For now, I want you to deeply appreciate the fact that salvation and redemption through Jesus have brought us to a place we could never have achieved by ourselves. This is a place Adam and Eve never enjoyed. Please keep all of this in mind as we consider more aspects of Jesus being both God and man. There must be a reason beyond what most Christians have discovered for Jesus going to such extremes to make us more than we could have ever been without Him. Could this have anything to do with us sharing in His ministry? I believe it does. And this has a profound influence on how we view Him.

What I have carefully described in this chapter was and is His role as the Son of God. If Jesus had ceased to be the Son of God and was only the Son of man, none of what I have described would have been possible.

Chapter 3
His Role as The Son

The Book of John provides considerable insight into the relationship between Jesus and His Father while Jesus was on earth. It is easy to imagine their close relationship before Jesus was born in human flesh. But this passage describes the relationship after Jesus was a grown man.

> *Philip saith unto him, Lord, show us the Father, and it sufficeth us. Jesus saith unto him, Have I been so long time with you, and yet hast thou not known me, Philip? he that hath seen me hath seen the Father; and how sayest thou then, Show us the Father? Believest thou not that I am in the Father, and the Father in me? the words that I speak unto you I speak not of myself: but the Father that dwelleth in me, he doeth the works. (John 14:8-10)*

I will break this down into its major parts to assist in understanding what Jesus has revealed, both to Philip and us. The response from Jesus was rather complex.

First, Jesus said: *he that hath seen me hath seen the Father.*

Next, Jesus said: *I am in the Father, and the Father in me.*

Finally, Jesus said: *the words that I speak unto you I speak not of myself: but the Father that dwelleth in me, he doeth the works.*

Those three statements say a lot about the role of Jesus as the Son of God. Yet they also express a closeness between God and a man, which was unheard of previously. It seems hard to grasp how Jesus could be in the Father and the Father could be in Him, at the same time. However, this is a scriptural concept that includes us as well.

At that day ye shall know that I am in my Father, and ye in me, and I in you. (John 14:20)

This is our reality. It is incumbent on us to increase the level of our understanding regarding these ideas. To help us do this, I will devote one chapter to each part of the statements made by Jesus. If it appears that I am moving back and forth from one point to another, it will be a purposeful movement. These thoughts are complex, and it is difficult to deal with them without reminding you of previous statements.

I will begin with the words: *he that hath seen me hath seen the Father.* When we see a baby boy, we commonly remark, "he looks just like his father." Naturally, we are speaking of a natural, physical resemblance. Jesus was not.

His Role as The Son

Jesus was speaking of a great deal more than this. There was a lot more at stake. It must have been shocking to His disciples. Absolutely no one dared to think or speak this way.

Jesus made it obvious that He was a man, just like those around Him. However, He also found it necessary to clearly distinguish the ways in which He was different. This difference can only be expressed by stating that Jesus was and still is both God and man. Jesus was a man, but Jesus was also the Son of God. This was something that could not be overlooked.

As hard as this is for us to understand, can you imagine how difficult it was for the members of His family? What about His earthly father? I can't imagine that Joseph did not struggle with this. Joseph was His father. But Jesus said more about His Father God than He ever said about Joseph. If it is more than you can grasp at the moment, there is nothing wrong with that. Keep reading.

There is no doubt that the fact Jesus was both God and man affected His ministry. **What is in question is how much of the ministry of Jesus took place because He was the Son of God.** I cannot stress this enough. Jesus always has been, and He always will be, the Son of God. There is no greater evidence of this than the words spoken at His water baptism.

And suddenly a voice came from heaven, saying, "This is My beloved Son, in whom I am well pleased." (Matthew 3:17 – NKJV)

On another occasion, when Jesus and three of His disciples were on the Mount of Transfiguration, while Jesus was speaking, Peter interrupted Him. Peter was inclined to do this. Peter was a man filled with curiosity, and he had no fear of making himself vulnerable if it meant he could get his answers. But this time, once again, the Father spoke from Heaven. Here is this part of the story.

> *Now after six days Jesus took Peter, James, and John his brother, led them up on a high mountain by themselves; and He was transfigured before them. His face shone like the sun, and His clothes became as white as the light. And behold, Moses and Elijah appeared to them, talking with Him. Then Peter answered and said to Jesus, "Lord, it is good for us to be here; if You wish, let us make here three tabernacles: one for You, one for Moses, and one for Elijah." While he was still speaking, behold, a bright cloud overshadowed them; and suddenly a voice came out of the cloud, saying, "This is My beloved Son, in whom I am well pleased. Hear Him!" (Matthew 17:1-5 – NKJV)*

It would be more than irresponsible to speak about Jesus being a man and completely ignore these two witnesses sent by His Heavenly Father. These two men, Moses and Elijah, had been in Heaven for many years. Yet, they obviously had some type of body that must have seemed very normal to Peter. He appears to be confident they would have no problem living on this earth once again. The spiritual nature and the physical nature of both men were evident. They were not both God and man. I am not implying that they were. They were only men. Yet, this seems to convey something significant about the nature of Jesus.

Nothing you will read in this book should be taken as a contradiction to what is found in these verses. These statements by the Father reinforce my argument that Jesus was both completely God and completely man.

Jesus did not need to quit being God to accomplish what we needed Him to do. He was our substitute, and He was, and He is our example. Whenever I have spoken about this, I have found a great deal of agreement on those issues.

It is the matter of the ministry of Jesus being conducted by a man that poses the problem. This need not be a problem if it is properly understood. No matter how much I may stress His humanity, it is never to demean His divinity. It is for the sole purpose of understanding how Jesus accomplished the works we are instructed to do.

If that baffles you a little, don't be too concerned. It baffles every person who attempts to deal with it.

Try wrapping your mind around the fact that even though you are just as human as you have ever been, as a Christian, you are as much a child of God as Jesus has ever been. You are completely human, and yet you are also completely a child of God.

You did not need to quit being a human to get saved. Thank God for that! It would mean none of us are saved.

Perhaps that will help you find the balance in what I am speaking about. You are both a human being and a spiritual being. Think of Jesus in a similar fashion.

In His teaching, Jesus claimed to be one with God and that God was His Father. This was precisely the point Jesus made in His conversation with Philip. I will admit that when these concepts are combined with the things He did, this causes many to attribute the healings and miracles Jesus performed to the divine part of His makeup. I am absolutely convinced this is not correct.

On more than one occasion, I have stated that this may be a matter of convenience. However, I am more inclined to think it results from a lack of revelation. The more I study the Bible, the more I realize there is more truth we do not yet understand than truth we truly grasp. Jesus being both God and man may be one of the greatest areas where we need more revelation. I believe it would be helpful to us in our relationship with God. It would also open our understanding of the exciting task to which we have been assigned.

We do not meet ordinary people who heal all the sick people they meet. Our hospitals are filled, and more are being built every day. Billions upon billions of dollars are spent on medicine and the care provided by the doctors. We are grateful for the availability of this medical help. At the same time, we understand the limitations of what the doctors and the hospitals can provide. New medicines are advertised all the time. Yet, it seems that many of them have the potential to do more harm than good.

Most of us who believe in Jesus and know about the things He did during His earthly ministry have often longed for Him to walk this earth again. That does not bother me, even though I understand the reason behind this way of thinking. We tend to view Him as capable of doing things we don't think we can do. And we usually attribute this to the fact He was, and He is the Son of God.

For anyone to come to a place where they believe they can do the works of Jesus is a growth process. It does not come overnight. Much of this is due to wrong ideas that have permeated the doctrines of the church.

We can be very Biblical until something we find uncomfortable is expected of us. We like to claim that we have a Biblical worldview. Do we embrace that view? That Biblical worldview must include doing the things Jesus did.

Jesus was God's Son. You, too, are God's child. I am God's child. We are not members of the Trinity. We never have been, and we never will be. But since Jesus has made us who we are, why don't we think more about who we are when we see people in need? This is exactly what Jesus did. The first major point Jesus made in His answer to Philip was to make it clear that He knew who He was.

Jesus said: *he that hath seen me hath seen the Father*. Just pretend for a moment that we should think of ourselves in a similar fashion. Most Christians would not dare to think of themselves in this way. Yet, the Bible says we are made in His image and likeness. Think about it!

We must know who we are. And if Jesus touched the lives of hurting people because He was God's child, why can't we do the same thing? I am declaring that we can, we should, and we must!

If we are going to grapple with this issue successfully, we cannot ignore the God part of Jesus. I realize that is a very awkward way to say this, but it seems more in line with how many people think. They tend to see a human side to Jesus, and they tend to see a God side to Jesus. Our natural minds just can't seem to grasp the fact that Jesus was both. Maybe it is because we think of ourselves as completely human, but we don't have the same view of our spirit being. Some of us have been taught that we are spiritually incomplete. Yet this is not what the Bible says.

> *And Let your ·patience [perseverance; endurance] show itself perfectly in what you do [have its full effect; finish its work]. Then you will be ·perfect and complete [mature and whole; or completely mature] and will ·have everything you need [lack nothing]. (James 1:4 – EXB)*

There is no doubt this speaks of spiritual completeness.

This will never happen to the human body. However, it does seem to be the goal for some people. Yet their bodies and minds age just like everybody else. So, am I suggesting we can reach a place where we never sin? Absolutely not!

I am only trying to show you that we have much more going for us on the positive side than we have working against us on the negative side. It is past time for us to embrace this.

Jesus is still completely God and completely man. He spent a great deal of time talking about this. So, I am spending a lot of time writing about it. It is my desire that you not only accept this by faith but that you grow in your ability to share it correctly and effectively with others.

Jesus knew these ideas would be difficult to understand and, therefore, difficult to believe. Yet we must believe this about Jesus because of what it says about us. We are very human. We all know that. It is obvious. At the same time, there are many places where the Bible talks about us as though we have two natures. To help us understand this better, we should examine some scriptural examples of what I have just stated about Jesus being the Son of God. It goes without question that Jesus did make these claims. The problem is not that Jesus said these things. How we understand and interpret them in the earthly life of Jesus is at issue. I will remind you once again of our Scriptures.

> *Jesus saith unto him, Have I been so long time with you, and yet hast thou not known me, Philip? he*

> *that hath seen me hath seen the Father; and how sayest thou then, Show us the Father? Believest thou not that I am in the Father, and the Father in me? the words that I speak unto you I speak not of myself: but the Father that dwelleth in me, he doeth the works. Believe me that I am in the Father, and the Father in me: or else believe me for the very works' sake. (John 14:9-11)*

Jesus claimed that since Philip had seen Him, he had also seen the Father. We could think that Jesus was speaking of His physical appearance. However, the words that follow let us know this was not the intended meaning behind these statements. Jesus was talking about the things He had been doing. He spoke of all His actions, the words He shared, and the message they contained. At the same time, Jesus provided this significant insight. *I am in the Father, and the Father in me.* Jesus challenged Philip to believe this by putting it in the form of this question.

Believest thou not that I am in the Father, and the Father in me? Jesus believed that Philip knew about this. But we should ask why this was so important. What was it about believing this that would make a difference in the life of Philip? For that matter, what is it about this question that is so important to us?

Is it possible that in our view of Jesus as a man, we tend to disconnect Him from His oneness with His Father? I think we do. And I also think this is what bothers us so much. We want to think of Jesus as God in the flesh. We tend not to want Jesus to be as human as we are. Our human frailty gets in the way. Thus, we don't see the man Jesus for who He was.

It is not that this is entirely wrong. It is just incomplete. Perhaps the best I can do is tell you they are two different beings. Yes, I do mean Jesus is both completely God and completely man. But even in His human body, as a total man, Jesus declared Himself to be one with God the Father.

If I wrote 10,000 pages on this subject, I could not fully explain it. No one can. We can only discuss it and try to grasp a few of the wonderful things this means. Our challenge is that nothing that is normal to us is also two different beings. At least, that is the way we tend to think.

There is nothing else like this that we know anything about. **That is nothing but us.** This is the transformative power of being born again, a concept that distinguishes the Christian life from the life of a follower of a false religion. When they embraced their religion, nothing about them changed. When we embraced Jesus, our entire world changed. This is a source of inspiration and hope. Consider these wonderful and powerful words.

> *I am crucified with Christ: nevertheless I live; yet not I, but Christ liveth in me: and the life which I now live in the flesh I live by the faith of the Son of God, who loved me, and gave himself for me. (Galatians 2:20)*

Could it be that much of our limitation in doing the works of Jesus is found in the fact that we do not view ourselves in this way? Let me ask some different questions. Do we see our relationship with God the same way Jesus saw His relationship with God? Would we dare to make such a claim as this? I think we should. I think this is God's plan. I think we must. Jesus taught us to call God our Father. Yet I have been shocked as I have noticed that very few people really think of God in this way.

Even if we do utter the words Jesus spoke, *he that hath seen me hath seen the Father,* we still have a hesitancy to apply that statement to ourselves in the same way Jesus did. There will be those who will read this book and be afraid to say these words really apply to them.

I can think of only one reason for feeling this way. It all lies in our relationship with Jesus. It seems clear to me that there was a reason Jesus said so many things about His relationship with His Father. He was demonstrating that relationship to us so that He could show us what is possible in our relationship with our Father. His plan was for His demonstration to create a desire in us for the same relationship.

This has happened in my heart. I hope the same thing has happened to you. If not, then I pray that it will. We are not robots to be used by God. Everything we do, good or bad, is a reflection of the condition of our personal relationship with our Heavenly Father.

His Role as The Son

Paul had a great deal to say about the people at Corinth's relationship with God. If you know anything about this group of people, then you know they were very carnal. Gross sin was common among them. Thus, Paul's words are filled with pointed and powerful instructions.

And I, brethren, could not speak unto you as unto spiritual, but as unto carnal, even as unto babes in Christ. I have fed you with milk, and not with meat: for hitherto ye were not able to bear it, neither yet now are ye able. For ye are yet carnal: for whereas there is among you envying, and strife, and divisions, are ye not carnal, and walk as men? For while one saith, I am of Paul; and another, I am of Apollos; are ye not carnal? Who then is Paul, and who is Apollos, but ministers by whom ye believed, even as the Lord gave to every man? I have planted, Apollos watered; but God gave the increase. So then neither is he that planteth anything, neither he that watereth; but God that giveth the increase. Now he that planteth and he that watereth are one: and every man shall receive his own reward according to his own labour. For we are labourers together with God: ye are God's husbandry, ye are God's building. According to the grace of God which is given unto me, as a wise masterbuilder, I have laid the foundation, and another buildeth thereon. But let every man take heed how he buildeth thereupon. For other foundation can no man lay than that is laid, which is Jesus Christ. (1 Corinthians 3:1-11)

I have witnessed Christians falter in their relationship with God because another better-known Christian failed. This should not happen. We have a very personal relationship with God. Therefore, we must ensure that our relationship with God is so solid and unshakeable that nothing can disrupt it. This security is only possible as we grow in our understanding of the Word.

Chapter 4
His Unity with His Father

Jesus told Philip that those who had seen Him had seen His Father. As we know so well, we can look like another person yet be nothing like them. Appearances can be deceiving. I know that would not be possible with Jesus and the Father, but Jesus wanted His message to be abundantly clear. Jesus was not just telling Philip that He looked like His Father. He was saying much more.

If Jesus had thoughts like these, He must have wondered what kind of statement would express His unity with His Father. The words Jesus spoke are something I would have never thought to say. I am speaking of these words which Jesus expressed very clearly. *I am in the Father, and the Father in me.*

As if that was not strong enough, Jesus continued to say: *the words that I speak unto you I speak not of myself: but the Father that dwelleth in me, he doeth the works.* I will have much more to share with you about those last statements. But I will tell you now, if you only speak your Father's words, that is a remarkable unity. But Jesus went even further and added the statement that the Father was dwelling in Him. How could that be possible?

By this point in time, I would imagine that the disciples' minds were about to explode. Who talked about God like this? Certainly, it was not anybody they had ever known. Yet here, Jesus stood right in front of them, making these bold statements about this incredible unity He had with God. They knew who God was, but this was quite different.

Jesus was determined for Philip to see that there was a powerful and inseparable unity between Him and His Father. I assume this was not just for Philip's sake. Jesus knew what was coming in a few short months. He knew this unity would be needed between Him and His disciples. They were going to need to continue without Him being visible to them. They needed this closeness with the Father.

In these statements, we can begin to see the necessary connection that will allow the flow of God's power to be transferred to and through us. There must be a powerful and inseparable unity between us and our Heavenly Father if we expect to be used by the Lord in ministering to others.

Those ideas may be enough to cause some to falter. But I am trying to help you move forward, not backward. So, it is fine to ask this question. Do you mean I can be a conduit

His Unity With His Father

through which the power of God can be transmitted to others? Yes, that is exactly what I mean. That is precisely what Jesus wanted Philip and the other disciples to understand.

One of my objectives in writing books is to cause my readers to desire a closer relationship with our Heavenly Father. I am not suggesting that we think of ourselves as gods. That would be ludicrous. I am proposing a closer relationship with God than most people believe is possible. The Psalmist wrote these words about unity.

Behold, how good and how pleasant it is for brethren to dwell together in unity! (Psalm 133:1)

The Hebrew word for unity is yahad.[8] According to the *Brown-Driver-Briggs Hebrew Lexicon*, this word means together. It may well be that when Jesus spoke of the closeness between Him and His Father, He was concerned they would take the unity in their relationship much too lightly. Perhaps that was His motivation for these rather strong and unusual statements.

What I have found so intriguing about this part of my study is the level of concern Jesus had regarding how the people viewed His relationship with His Father.

Now, don't take this concern as a worry. Jesus knew He would not be healing people and doing miracles as the Son of God. But the closeness Jesus had with His Father tremendously influenced what Jesus did as a man.

Jesus was going to heal the sick, cleanse lepers, and raise the dead, and then tell His disciples to do the same things they saw Him do. Jesus had to do these things as a man. Otherwise, His disciples would not be able to repeat what Jesus was doing. At the same time, Jesus could not allow Himself to only be seen as a man.

Jesus had to make it clear He was the Son of God. Then, He had to make it clear that nothing had changed between Him and His Father. They were as close and as united as they had ever been. Jesus had another concern, and it was the relationships between His disciples. Those relationships needed to be close. They needed to be close with each other, and they needed to be close with Him. His disciples needed the same relationship Jesus had with His Father. And this is precisely what Jesus desires for us today.

At the opposite extreme of what I have just suggested is where you will find most Christians. A common statement is that a person does not feel close to God. They may want to know how to feel closer to God. These thoughts should never enter our minds. We should know what the Bible says about our relationship with God, and we should believe it. When we see ourselves the way God sees us, this closeness is never an issue. He said He would never leave us nor forsake us.

The late Fanny Crosby penned a hymn many years ago that expresses this desire to be closer to God. You may know the song and may have sung it as often as I did before I knew any better. It is much more emotional than it is truthful.

As well-intentioned as Fanny Crosby must have been, her song is not Scripturally correct. The chorus says: "Draw me nearer, nearer, nearer, blessed Lord, to the cross where Thou hast died; draw me nearer, nearer, nearer, blessed Lord, to thy precious, bleeding side."[9] Jesus has risen from the dead. His side is not bleeding!

More importantly, James made it clear in his letter that drawing near to God does not begin with God. It begins with us. He did not stop there. James went on to tell us what is involved in drawing near to God.

Draw near to God and He will draw near to you. Cleanse your hands, you sinners; and purify your hearts, you double-minded. (James 4:8 – NKJV)

Only when we take the first steps in drawing nearer to God will he draw near to us! The power to have or not have this unity I have written about rests with us.

By no means am I trying to be offensive. Yet, I wonder at times just how offensive we are to our Heavenly Father. The notion of not feeling close to God seems to contradict much of what the New Testament says about us. You may remember that the Apostle Paul wrote these words.

God, who made the world and everything in it, since He is Lord of heaven and earth, does not dwell in temples made with hands. Nor is He worshiped with men's hands, as though He needed anything,

> *since He gives to all life, breath, and all things. And He has made from one blood every nation of men to dwell on all the face of the earth, and has determined their preappointed times and the boundaries of their dwellings, so that they should seek the Lord, in the hope that they might grope for Him and find Him, though He is not far from each one of us; for in Him we live and move and have our being, as also some of your own poets have said, 'For we are also His offspring.'*
> (Acts 17:24-28 – NKJV)

The progression in these verses is brilliant. I especially like Paul's statements about the Lord being *not far from each one of us*. Then he immediately proceeds to say *in Him we live and move and have our being*. It seems clear that Paul thought of his relationship with God in the same way Jesus did. So why shouldn't we do the same?

To say that Jesus is the very essence of our life is to express a closeness that many people don't seem to experience. That is sad, yet it also explains a great deal about the way many Christians live. They are more than a little disconnected from the relationship the Bible tells us we should have with the Lord Jesus.

I will take this concept of a close and even intimate relationship with God a few steps further. I have mentioned that Jesus said: *but the Father that dwelleth in me, he doeth the works*. What did Jesus mean by that statement?

Let's begin with the words: *the Father that dwelleth in me.* I have written a few words about this, but there is more. If you have not experienced the kind of closeness to God that I have written about, read over all of this again. Read it slowly and let it all sink in. A great relationship with your Heavenly Father awaits you.

When Jesus was teaching His disciples about the Holy Spirit, He made several statements that have not been well understood. It is much too easy to gloss over them and not allow them to be meaningful. Jesus was not just speaking to His disciples. He was also speaking to us. This is the passage of which I speak.

> *"If you love me, keep my commands. And I will ask the Father, and he will give you another advocate to help you and be with you forever— the Spirit of truth. The world cannot accept him because it neither sees him nor knows him. But you know him, for he lives with you and will be in you. I will not leave you as orphans; I will come to you. Before long, the world will not see me anymore, but you will see me. Because I live, you also will live. On that day you will realize that I am in my Father, and you are in me, and I am in you. (John 14:15-20 – NIV)[10]*

Jesus said His disciples knew the Spirit of truth. Do you know the Spirit of truth? In those few statements, recorded by John, Jesus drew a line between those who know the Father and those who do not. He stated very clearly that the *world* cannot receive the Holy Spirit. Consider this to be a reference to the unity and the close relationship I have been writing about in the previous paragraphs.

We can base this conclusion on the fact that Jesus made it equally clear who would know and receive the Spirit. Immediately after that, we find these amazing words regarding the Holy Spirit.

But you know him, for he lives with you and will be in you. Once again, we are confronted with this seemingly strange type of relationship. It exudes (displays conspicuously) a closeness that many know nothing about. And to make things more interesting, Jesus concluded His remarks with these words. *On that day you will realize that I am in my Father, and you are in me, and I am in you.*

Being filled with the Holy Spirit is so much more than many Pentecostal Christians seem to understand. Yes, we should speak in tongues. Yes, we should be used in the nine gifts of the Holy Spirit. But most of all, it should be obvious that the Holy Spirit lives in us. I am convinced this should be obvious without us making mention of it.

This is further evidence that when Jesus spoke of His unity with the Father, He intended for it to extend beyond them. The ultimate goal was for this unity to extend throughout the ages to every person who comes to know Jesus as Lord and Savior.

Chapter 5
His Words - His Works

Continuing the discussion of the conversation Jesus had with Philip necessitates another look at the Scriptures on which I have based my statements. Remember, this was a direct and very personal conversation between Jesus and Philip. Of course, there were other people present to hear what was said.

> *Philip saith unto him, Lord, show us the Father, and it sufficeth us. Jesus saith unto him, Have I been so long time with you, and yet hast thou not known me, Philip? he that hath seen me hath seen the Father; and how sayest thou then, Show us the Father? Believest thou not that I am in the Father, and the Father in me? the words that I speak unto you I speak not of myself: but the Father that dwelleth in me, he doeth the works. (John 14:8-10)*

After declaring that any person who had seen Jesus had seen the Father, the conversation was taken to a deeper level.

Jesus went on to say: *the words that I speak unto you I speak not of myself.* Jesus was telling Philip His words were not His own words. This was one way Jesus expressed how close His relationship was with His Father. I know these statements may seem too obvious to belabor them as I am doing. However, many may have ignored the significance of what Jesus said to Philip. It was not a light and frivolous conversation. We can benefit a great deal from what was said.

My suggestion is based on the next phrase. Jesus added these words: *but the Father that dwelleth in me, he doeth the works.* In a matter of just a few words, Jesus made a strong connection between Him speaking the **words** of His Father and His Father doing the **works** they had witnessed. We should think about those statements very carefully.

The underlying theme of this book is that we should be doing the same things Jesus did. Jesus gave us that assignment. So, if we are going to do these things, I believe it is essential to know how Jesus did them. Remember that we cannot separate the way Jesus was able to do things from who He was. When Jesus asked His disciples about the public perception the people had, He was stressing His humanity and its importance.

No matter who you are, there will always be a direct connection between your words and how you perceive yourself. But there must also be a direct connection between your words and **His works**. Our words either place a limit on what He does, or they extend both the nature and the volume

His Words – His Works

of what He does. Jesus made this connection in His life and ministry. We must do the same. This is a key factor in doing the works of Jesus. Sadly, we have often allowed our self-image to keep us from doing what God has called us to do.

If I desire for the Father to do the work that needs to be done, then I must speak only His words. I will not be inclined to do that unless I know who I am. I will hesitate to such a degree that I will miss many opportunities to witness the works my Father desires to do.

When I place my hands on a sick person and expect God to heal them, I need to speak the right words. But it is equally important for me to have the correct self-image. The only right words are **His words**. This is because God will be doing **His work**. The only correct self-image is seeing myself the way God sees me.

I should listen to God before I say or do anything. Since this was so important to Jesus, it must be important to me. He made numerous efforts to communicate this to those who followed Him. Most of those who were with Him did not grasp this. And most of those who love Him and live for Him today still do not grasp this truth.

When I minister to people who are sick, I must not just be saying words I have heard other people say. I should never be making up words to say because I think they sound good or they make me sound like I know what I am doing. Jesus never did that, and neither should I.

Every time I minister to a sick person by laying my hands on them as Jesus prescribed, I am expecting God to heal them. If they are blind, I expect them to see. If they have cancer, I expect the cancer to die. When I say I expect these things to happen, please understand that I am basing my expectations on what God has promised. I consider the promises found in the Bible to be promises that God has made to me.

Since I am expecting God to do these things, doesn't it seem reasonable that I should be quiet and listen to what God is saying? This is what Jesus did. Why would I interrupt what God wants to say? Are my words as important as His?

**God is doing the works.
Therefore, we should only speak God's words.**

One of our great problems is saying one thing and yet doing another. God never does that. Jesus never did that. But we do. We have had this tendency to say something that we think sounds good, but we may expect nothing to happen. I know that is true because I have seen and heard it many times. This may be the source of our failure to open the door for our Father to do the works we desire to see.

It is not likely that you or I will always say words that we hear God speak. I know that. We are not perfect. And I am not attempting to cause you to think that you can or should live that way. The world would become a different place if we all behaved in this way. That would be wonderful.

Jesus expressed a clear connection between the **words** He heard His Father speak and the **works** His Father did. This should have a great deal to do with what happens when we lay our hands on the sick. Yet, I must admit that I have never heard anyone else describe what I have just written in the way I have shared it with you. Surely, they have, and I was not privy to it, but now you are.

If this is beginning to seem repetitious, be assured that it is being done on purpose. I am repeating this concept in different ways so that it will stick in your mind and you will not forget it. I consider the understanding God has given me regarding the relationship between what we say and what God does to be one of the most treasured things the Holy Spirit has taught me.

We may be following the instructions of Jesus by placing our hands on a sick person and praying for them. But what do we use to determine what we say? Often, I think we only repeat what we have heard other people say. What if we said nothing until or unless our Heavenly Father spoke to us and gave us words to say?

Shouldn't this same approach apply to the working of miracles? I know this is listed as one of the gifts of the Spirit.[11] However, I am also aware there seems to be extraordinarily little understanding of what we are supposed to do to work a miracle. Not doing what I suggested in the previous paragraphs may be why we have not seen much of the miraculous.

We rely too much on our own words.

Another translation of the verses we are discussing is worded in this way.

> *Jesus said to him, "Have I been with you so long, and you still do not know me, Philip? Whoever has seen me has seen the Father. How can you say, 'Show us the Father'? Do you not believe that I am in the Father and the Father is in me? The words that I say to you I do not speak on my own authority, but the Father who dwells in me does his works. Believe me that I am in the Father and the Father is in me, or else believe on account of the works themselves. (John 14:9-11 – ESV)[12]*

When the translators of the old King James Version of the Bible translated verse ten of this passage, they indicated that Jesus said: *the words that I speak unto you I speak not of myself.* A casual reading of those words leaves one with the notion that Jesus only stated that He was not the source of His words. This is helpful, but it does not provide the insight we have in this second translation.

According to the translators of the English Standard Version of the New Testament, Jesus said: *The words that I say to you I do not speak on my own authority.* What Jesus wanted to convey was much more than Him not being the source of His words. All works of significance require the authority to make them happen.

Where, how, and when do we expect to get this authority? Is this a blanket authority that applies to every person in every situation? **It is not**, or we would have seen more of these works. If that were the case, I am not sure Jesus would have made these statements. If we all had this authority and knew how to use it, then it would not have been necessary for Jesus to say what He said.

There is a necessary connection between the words that are spoken and the works we are expecting. This authority I am writing about permeates both the words and the works.

The Father's authority is the connection between the words and the works. This makes it essential that the words and the works emanate (originate from or be produced) by the Father. All the authority we have was given to us by Him. I have heard a great deal about the believer's authority but not much about the Father's authority.

However, for the moment, I want to couch all of this in the **necessity of the relationship** between Jesus and His Father. The works that Jesus did were the result of this close relationship between Jesus and His Father. It was a relationship so close that Jesus relied on His Father for the very words He spoke.

The authority Jesus used to repeat the words His Father gave to Him also came from His Father. When the right conditions were met, His Father did the works. As you can see, it becomes almost impossible to determine who is saying what and who is doing what. Was it Jesus, or was it the Father? We can't tell, and this is exactly the way it is supposed to be.

There should never be any doubt regarding who will receive the glory for the works that are accomplished. If this ever becomes an issue, it is due to the lack of this close relationship. It means the attention has shifted to the person ministering and away from the Father. This has happened much too often, and it always stops the flow of the Holy Spirit.

I am speaking of a lifestyle. This way of living does not happen automatically. It is the result of time spent in the Word of God and in the presence of our Heavenly Father. The lifestyle I am speaking of may take longer for some to develop than it does for others. Much of this depends on the religious influence and erroneous beliefs instilled in an individual from birth. For some with no religious upbringing, this close relationship may be easier and may be formed quickly.

I am writing about a statement Jesus made more than once. Thus, it is especially important to pay close attention to it and understand it. All His words were important. But when Jesus took the time to repeat Himself, we know these were thoughts and expressions of truth He desired for those who followed Him to receive and understand. To do the works Jesus did requires us to do things the way Jesus did them.

Here is another example of Jesus expressing these same ideas. I have included two different versions for you to ponder.

His Words – His Works

For I have not spoken of myself; but the Father which sent me, he gave me a commandment, what I should say, and what I should speak.
(John 12:49 - KJV)

For I have not spoken on my own authority, but the Father who sent me has himself given me a commandment—what to say and what to speak.
(John 12:49 – ESV)[13]

Now, let's shift our attention to the matter of power and authority. From the statements I have made, one might get the idea that I am saying that Jesus did not even have the authority to choose His own words. If that is true, then should we question the ability Jesus had to do other things?

In these statements from John, it sounds like all the power and authority had remained in Heaven when Jesus came to earth. Is this true? Did Jesus have no power of His own? Was Jesus only a conduit for the power His Father had? Was Jesus sent to this earth to do the will of His Father and yet He was not given the necessary power to do it?

This was not the case. It makes me cringe to write these questions. In His own words, Jesus lets us know this was not the case. He had all the power and authority He needed.

And Jesus came and spake unto them, saying, All power is given unto me in heaven and in earth.
(Matthew 28:18)

Combining those words with what I have just written causes me to have many other questions. If Jesus had the power, why didn't He just do the works? Does this involve more than power? Was there another purpose involved, and if so, is that a valid purpose today? Could these things be our problem?

We do tend to talk like all that we need is more power. And we act as though the only purpose of having that power is to get the results. I think this is a huge problem!

I can't read those words from Matthew 28:18 and not ask this question. If this power was given to Jesus to do the things He did, then has that same power been given to us? I have heard many people answer that question with a resounding yes! But if that is true, then why don't we see more of the things that power produced in the life of Jesus?

Much of that answer is found in our reliance on our own words. Instead of waiting to hear what the Father wants us to say, we just start talking. Another part of the answer could be that we rely on our power rather than the power Jesus spoke about. If we honestly believe that the same power given to Jesus has also been given to us, then we should never have this conflict.

Often, Jesus would be certain He had listened to His Father for instructions before He healed people or performed a miracle. This kind of conversation is the prayer Jesus prayed before He raised Lazarus from the dead.

Then they took away the stone from the place where the dead man was lying. And Jesus lifted up His eyes and said, "Father, I thank You that You have heard Me. And I know that You always hear Me, but because of the people who are standing by I said this, that they may believe that You sent Me." Now when He had said these things, He cried with a loud voice, "Lazarus, come forth!" And he who had died came out bound hand and foot with graveclothes, and his face was wrapped with a cloth. Jesus said to them, "Loose him, and let him go."
(John 11:41-45 – NKJV)

Jesus wanted the people who were watching Him to know that He had spoken to His Father about what He was going to do. The kind of relationship Jesus had with His Father that is illustrated in this story about Lazarus is so important in doing the works of Jesus.

This conversation recorded in John 11:41-45 between Jesus and His Father about raising Lazarus from the dead may have contained much more information than we have in these Scriptures. I am confident that it did. But at least this story of Jesus raising Lazarus from the dead is specific evidence that Jesus did communicate with His Father before He performed miracles and healed the sick.

Conversations like I have mentioned were not limited to what took place between Jesus and the Father. What we find mentioned in the Gospel of Mark indicates that conversations of a similar nature occurred between Jesus and the disciples before Jesus returned to Heaven. Jesus gave clear instructions to the disciples and told them that great signs and wonders would follow them. We can see this in these very precise instructions given by Jesus.

> *And these signs shall follow them that believe; In my name shall they cast out devils; they shall speak with new tongues; They shall take up serpents; and if they drink any deadly thing, it shall not hurt them; they shall lay hands on the sick, and they shall recover. So then after the Lord had spoken unto them, he was received up into heaven, and sat on the right hand of God. And they went forth, and preached everywhere, the Lord working with them, and confirming the word with signs following. Amen. (Mark 16:17-20)*

I have heard many things said about the last part of this passage. Some do not believe it should be included in our Bible. I disagree. These statements do belong in our Bible. On the other hand, if I did not believe in doing the things Jesus said to do, I might want to exclude these instructions, too. But as I was writing, this thought occurred to me. Just as the Father had been collaborating with Jesus and confirming the words He had spoken through Jesus, now Jesus was doing the same thing with His disciples.

Jesus publicly claimed He was saying things His Father told Him to say. The proof of this was the miracles and healings. Now, the disciples were saying things and claiming they had received their message from Jesus. The proof this was true came through the signs that followed the disciples.

Some prominent people say that signs, wonders, healings, and miracles have all stopped. They are wrong. Just because they don't believe we can do the works of Jesus; it doesn't make it so. I have witnessed too many miracles and have seen too many people healed to fall for that nonsense.

The next step in this Heaven-to-earth communication is the one that is often missed. Those who believe that signs and wonders and miracles and healings have ceased must also believe God has stopped speaking. **These do go together.** Are we supposed to believe that God does not talk to us? I certainly don't believe that. My Father and I talk almost every day. And it is my fault if a day goes by, and we don't talk. I just got too busy. But God is always available when I want to talk to Him.

Maybe those with a cessation mentality think the way they do because God has stopped speaking to them. I do realize those are strong words. But they do seem to be reasonable. Why would God speak to anyone about performing a miracle if they did not believe it would happen? God knows what we believe. Honestly, I believe God does talk to people like I have described. The real problem is that they just don't listen to Him.

When Jesus gave the promise of the Holy Spirit, He revealed a wonderful set of facts. They describe a relationship between the Holy Spirit and the person in whom He dwells that is remarkably similar to the relationships I have just described. Read this very carefully. It was written for you.

> *I have many things to say unto you, but ye cannot bear them now. Howbeit when he, the Spirit of truth, is come, he will guide you into all truth: for he shall not speak of himself; but whatsoever he shall hear, that shall he speak: and he will shew you things to come. He shall glorify me: for he shall receive of mine, and shall shew it unto you. All things that the Father hath are mine: therefore said I, that he shall take of mine, and shall shew it unto you. (John 16:12-14)*

The first audience to hear these words was comprised of the disciples. The book of Acts records many stories of what happened because of this relationship between the Holy Spirit and the believer. This relationship continues today, making it possible for us to do the works that Jesus did.

These are His works. We are only the hands He uses to conduct what He wants to do. We must listen carefully to what Jesus has told the Holy Spirit to tell us to say and do. It is His words that Jesus is confirming with signs following. The Holy Spirit is the agent living in us to oversee the delivery of the words and the manifestation of the works.

**God help us to listen, then obey
and then get out of the way.**

I will say it once more. We are too quick to speak our own words and ignore what the Holy Spirit attempts to convey. I have no doubt I have uncovered a major reason we do not see more signs and wonders. I do believe this will change. It must change!

Chapter 6
His Determination

It is reasonable to think of the Son of God only saying what His Father told Him to say. We would expect Him to be very guarded and careful about the words He spoke. I believe there was more to this than being careful not to say the wrong thing. It was the Father who was acting through Jesus, so it mattered that it was also the Father speaking through Jesus.

As I endeavored to explain these wonderful truths about the relationship between Jesus and His Father, I caught sight of something else that is just as thrilling. I will provide some quotes to help make this clear.

> *Verily, verily, I say unto you, He that believeth on me, the works that I do shall he do also; and greater works than these shall he do; because I go unto my Father. (John 14:12)*

> *Believe me that I am in the Father, and the Father in me: or else believe me for the very works' sake.*

> *Verily, verily, I say unto you, He that believeth on me, the works that I do shall he do also; and greater works than these shall he do; because I go unto my Father. And whatsoever ye shall ask in my name, that will I do, that the Father may be glorified in the Son. If ye shall ask anything in my name, I will do it. (John 14:11-14)*

Many times, I have quoted John 14:12, but I did not include the verse before it nor the two verses after it. Considering this as one whole unit paints a wonderful picture of the determination of Jesus. He clearly states what He desires. Then He proceeds to tell us exactly what we must do.

Jesus told His audience that He wanted them to believe what He said about His relationship with the Father. This would have been beneficial to them on a personal level. Also, it would have indicated a level of faith they had not previously expressed.

However, if they were not prepared to take this step for their benefit, He requested that they do it for those present who were sick. There were blind people who needed to receive their sight. Lepers needed to be cleansed.

**Jesus said,
"Believe what I am saying to you for their sake."**

Has it ever crossed your mind that what you believe or don't believe may have an impact on another person receiving what they need from Jesus? This was the point Jesus was making when He added these few words, *or else believe me for the very works' sake.*

Jesus must have been thinking about what had happened in His hometown. We do not know how many people never received the miracles they needed because of other people's unbelief in those meetings in Nazareth. What we do know is that Jesus was doing His best to make sure this did not happen again. It is time for Pastors, Teachers, and Evangelists to do what Jesus did. Why not be as bold as Jesus? It is time to speak up for the truth!

Why not tell our audiences they should believe that God still heals and does miracles today? It is selfish not to believe this. If they don't think God will do these things for them, then believe He does them for others. If they don't want to believe what God has said for themselves, then at least believe it for the benefit of others. That is precisely what Jesus was saying.

Unbelief can stop the miraculous! I am not trying to be melodramatic. Churches are filled with people with serious needs. I wonder how different this could be if we could rid our churches of unbelief. Is there any effort made to do this? I would say it is not happening. Why not? Why do we keep acting like the people in Nazareth? Surely, we know better.

What I have just shared with you is a new way of thinking. I had known for years that there was a problem, and

I knew the crowd had something to do with it. If you had asked me what I thought, I would have told you. My response would have been a repeat of what others were saying. I would have told you that we need to teach more people how to have faith and how to use it. People do need more faith.

However, you can't have faith and unbelief at the same time. We have been trying to get people who are saturated with unbelief to use faith they do not have. **The presence of unbelief is proof there is no faith.** The unbelief has replaced their faith. Of course, that statement assumes they did have faith. Many Christians are like the people Jesus spoke to when He made these statements. They had known who Jesus was for years, but they did not believe in Him.

Christianity has an abundance of people who are as I just described. They don't believe in what He can do because they don't know Jesus for who He is. This is a personal relationship. We do not inherit it from our parents. It only comes about because of a personal decision. And until that relationship decision is made, building a person up in faith is impossible.

I have done exactly what Jesus did. Often, He attacked what they did not believe. We tend to ignore what people don't believe. People will not have faith until they deal with what they don't believe. We are talking about changing minds!

Despite what many people who have taught faith seem to believe; you will never find faith and unbelief in the same person. They may say the right words and quote the right Scriptures. Their prayers may sound right. But the real test is found in the form of results. Not understanding this has confused many people.

Many of those who have taught the subject of faith have not understood how a person can meet **their criteria** for faith and not get results. Maybe it is time to reexamine that criteria. Why not use the criteria Jesus gave us? Jesus was never confused about why the people did not get healed or did not receive a miracle. It should not confuse us. No matter how much effort goes into concealing unbelief, it will eventually be exposed. Sadly, this usually comes when there is a great need for faith.

> I am determined to be
> as determined as Jesus.

Chapter 7
His Challenge to Us

Huge buildings packed full of unbelievers who claim to be Christians are dangerous places to be. The people may be laughing. They may be entertained. They may enjoy the music and the coffee. But if they don't believe Jesus is who He said He was and is, then nothing worthwhile is happening. What is taking place is much like a sedative. The people are being lulled into a deadly trance that will rob them of their health and their money. It will lead them to an early grave.

This will not only be true for those filled with unbelief, but it will also happen to many people in serious need of the power of God. This is the point Jesus was making. It is the point I have been making. But Jesus did not stop there. He gave us a statement that many have memorized and tried to use. I will provide the context.

> *Verily, verily, I say unto you, He that believeth on me, the works that I do shall he do also; and greater*

> *works than these shall he do; because I go unto my Father. And whatsoever ye shall ask in my name, that will I do, that the Father may be glorified in the Son. If ye shall ask anything in my name, I will do it. (John 14:12-14)*

Immediately after Jesus said that we can do the works that He did and even greater works, He provided an awesome promise. The promise clarifies that we are not expected to do these "works" on our own. We have tremendous help available. That help comes through prayer.

The Father and the Son are together. When we pray, they both can hear us. So, whatever we ask, using the name of Jesus, we have a promise that Jesus will do it. Jesus said that at least twice. Just keep one thing in mind. Jesus made this promise to provide opportunities to glorify His Father.

If you can collect all of this together in your thoughts, you will discover an amazing truth. Jesus started this conversation with a group of people who did not believe in Him. He knew that. So, what did Jesus proceed to do? He promised that if they asked God for something, He would hear them. Then, while still on earth, Jesus told them He would do what they asked.

That is throwing down the gauntlet! It is as though Jesus told them, "If you don't believe that I am who I said I am, let me prove it to you." "You talk to God, and I will provide the answer." Think about that for a moment!

His Challenge to Us

On the one hand, that is bold and may even seem to be an unusual risk. But it wasn't so for Jesus. He knew who He was, and He knew what He could do. This raises an important question.

What should we do when we are faced with people who are filled with unbelief? Why not follow the example Jesus gave us? I do not mean we should promise to do something they talked to God about, and we have no idea what they asked God to do. That could prove foolhardy, especially if we don't know what they asked for in prayer. On the other hand, it could prove to be immensely powerful if the gifts of the Spirit are in operation in our lives.

Has it occurred to you that in these statements, Jesus indicated that at least two of the gifts of the Spirit were in operation in His life? These were the gifts of the word of knowledge and the word of wisdom that Paul mentioned in *1 Corinthians chapter 12*. There are other stories about the ministry of Jesus where examples of these gifts are provided. I will talk about this in some of the later chapters of this book.

For right now, I am talking about something much more common for us. Jesus was proficient in all of the gifts of the Spirit. We may not be, so let's interject some wisdom.

When confronted with a person struggling with unbelief in one area, take them to a promise from the Word of God that deals with something else. Talk to them about their salvation if they are filled with unbelief regarding healing.

**That is the concept.
This is not a diversionary tactic.**

It is always best to work from the known to the unknown. What I am suggesting is a method to help them overcome their unbelief. If we can find common ground, then progress is possible. This is precisely what Jesus was doing. These were religious people. They had prayed many times, and God had answered their prayers. But Jesus healing sick people, opening blind eyes, and cleansing lepers was new to them. They had never seen anyone else do these things.

Jesus said to them, "You talk to God, and I will provide the answer." Nothing could beat that for proving that Jesus was who He claimed to be. What a novel idea. Brilliant!

Has it also occurred to you that by using this prayer that Jesus gave us in *John 14:12-14*, we can do what He did? Not only that, but it is also a method we have been given that we can use anytime there is a tinge of uncertainty. Stop what you are attempting to do and talk to God about it. He will answer.

Did you notice that Jesus did not say anything about our faith? I am not saying we don't need faith. Of course, we need faith. But keep in mind that Jesus did a lot of things to glorify His Father. And if unbelief was not blocking what He wanted to do, great things would happen. This may be a new way of thinking for you. If so, read the Gospels again.

Don't just accept unbelief. Do something about it.

His Challenge to Us

I was conducting a meeting in North Carolina a few years ago. I was at this church at the request of a wonderful man of God, who is now in Heaven. The pastor did not think I would come to his church because of the small size of his congregation, so he had a friend tell me he wanted me to come. This was one of the smallest crowds I have ever preached to, but it resulted in one of the most outstanding miracles I have ever witnessed. When I tell you what happened, you will know how thrilled I am that I went to this church.

A lady in the church knew a young man, perhaps nineteen years old, who had been shot in a drug deal that had gone wrong. This young man was not buying or selling the drugs. He was with the wrong crowd and was sitting in the back seat of the car when this incident occurred.

There was an argument between two guys about the drug deal. One guy was outside the car, and three guys were inside the car. The guy outside the car pulled out a gun and began shooting at the car. The young man I will tell you about was sitting in the back seat by himself. One bullet struck this young man in the spine, and other bullets hit him in several other areas. As a result, the young man was bent over at the waist and could not stand up straight. He was in a lot of pain. He also could not put his right heel down on the floor. He had been told he would be like this for the rest of his life.

When this incident happened, this young man did not know Jesus. He had never been to church. But, a few days before the start of my meeting, this pastor went to the hospital and led this young fellow to the Lord. Then, the pastor got special permission to pick this young man up and bring him to church, promising he would bring him back to the rehab part of the hospital after the meeting was over. I do not know how many days had passed before he came to one of my services.

When I stood up to teach that night, I saw this young man lying in a recliner at the back of the auditorium. The pastor had only told me parts of this story. I knew he would be there and could not sit in a regular chair. I shared my message and asked if anyone wanted me to pray for them. Two men brought this young guy to the front row. When I walked over to him, he was staring down at the floor. He was bent over at the waist, and he couldn't straighten up and sit up in the chair. He could not look up at me.

Unless God did something for him, this young man would be in this awful, contorted position for the rest of his life. That was everything I knew about him.

At first, I did not say anything to him. The Lord told me just to take him by the hands, so I asked him to give me his hands. I held his hands for a moment and did not say anything.

Suddenly, he jumped up out of the chair. He stood straight up and put his right foot flat on the floor. He had the most surprised look on his face that I have ever seen. All of this happened in a matter of less than two minutes.

His Challenge to Us

The entire time, I never said a word. I just stood there holding his hands.

When he jumped to his feet, he yelled, "I don't hurt anymore. I don't hurt anywhere." He pulled his hands out of mine and took off running. The auditorium was large enough to hold about three hundred people, but there were not that many chairs. He had lots of room to run, and he took full advantage of it. He ran around that auditorium several times.

As he ran around that auditorium, he shouted, "I can't believe it! I can't believe it!" I just stood and watched.

Was this unbelief? No. He had never been around people who believed in healing. He was expecting nothing. He did not know enough to have unbelief. He could have been disappointed if nothing happened. Disappointment is often a precursor to unbelief.

This was the working of miracles, one of the nine Gifts of the Spirit. This miracle did not require any faith on his part. But I want to stress that the absence of unbelief made it possible for the Holy Spirit to do this great miracle for this young man.

I have not had any contact with this fellow since that night. I know that the pastor did all he could to keep him in church and teach him the Word of God. He was that kind of Pastor and has now moved on to his Heavenly reward. I look forward to seeing him someday.

How did I know what to do? I listened for instructions from the Holy Ghost before I said or did anything. I only did what He told me to do. Let me say that again. I only did what the Holy Ghost told me to do. To God be all the glory.

Jesus challenged His disciples to do the same works that He did. All of them but Judas Iscariot accepted that challenge. We have several stories in the Bible about the results these eleven men enjoyed. We do not have any such stories about Judas Iscariot. The Early Church Fathers, as certain men are known, also recorded many stories about wonderful things that happened in the ministry of some of these men.

While all of these things are wonderful to read about, and they do encourage us, they should also provoke us. It was not the plan of God for all of this to end when Jesus returned to Heaven. What we have recorded in the Bible is just the stories of how it all began. It is now our responsibility to embrace the challenge Jesus gave those disciples who saw Him face to face.

I have only seen Jesus in a vision, and it was an amazing experience. But someday, I will see Him face to face. When I stand before Him, I want there to be no question about how I embraced His instructions. So, I encourage you to accept His challenge. He is ready to work through your life if you are willing for Him to do so. I encourage you to embrace His Challenge today!

Chapter 8
His Imitators

Listening to and then obeying the voice of the Holy Spirit is extremely important. This is a key factor in the way miracles and healings take place. Yet a greater issue could be the underlying purpose for these miracles and healings. It can often seem as though getting the miracle or the healing is all that matters to us. That should not be. I have seen God heal many people. Some of these people had terrible things wrong with them. We ministered to them and God healed them, and yet they never came to church again. That must be offensive to God. What a slap in the face of the one who suffered so much for our salvation and healing. God has a higher goal than just fixing what is wrong with this body.

That higher goal is a stronger relationship with God for the person who is healed or the one who receives the miracle. No matter how wonderful it might be to see a blind person healed or to see the lame walk and the dumb talk, if a closer relationship with God does not happen, we have failed.

I know those are strong words. But I know I am right.

I held a meeting a few years ago in a church in Pennsylvania. It was a great church with a wonderful pastor. The congregation was very committed and hungry to hear God's Word. One night of the meeting, as I was laying hands on people, I stood in front of a lady who did not look like she belonged in church.

This does not mean there is a dress code for what you should wear to church. It means there are certain things you don't wear to church if you respect the house of God. This woman looked like she had just walked out of a nightclub, and I don't mean she was dressed to be there as a patron. I would have guessed her to be a cocktail waitress or something much worse.

When I looked at her, I simply asked what she wanted God to do for her. Her answer surprised me. She said, "I don't know anything about your God. I have seriously injured my back, and I can no longer work because of the pain. They told me you can heal people. So, I came for you to heal me." With a response like that, I started asking more questions.

The woman said she was an exotic dancer, and she had hurt her back doing her routine. My next step was to ask her if she knew Jesus. I asked the question several different ways. Every time, her answer was no. Finally, I got straight to the point and asked her if she would like to get saved and live for Jesus. She said, "No, I don't have time for that religious stuff."

I said, "I am talking about you going to Heaven or Hell." Once again, she said, "I don't care about that stuff. I don't believe in it." Finally, I said: "If you don't care anything about my Jesus, why did you come here?"

The woman replied: "I need to work. I need the money. So quit talking to me about Jesus and heal me so I can return to work." Yes, she was that abrupt. I stood there quietly and waited to see what the Father said.

I heard the Father speak, and I said what He said. I looked her right straight in the eyes, and I said: "If you don't care anything about my Jesus, then why should He heal you?"

She was getting angrier by the minute. It was obvious. She looked at me and said: "Well if that's how you are going to be, I'll just leave." I said: "Suit yourself. Leave if you want to. But I can tell you that you need a lot more than getting your back healed so you can go back to doing your exotic dances. You need Jesus in your life!"

She went storming up the aisle and out the back door. I don't know what happened to her. I never saw her again. I hope she never forgot what she heard that night.

There is a purpose for healing, miracles, signs, and wonders. It has much more to do with the life to come than with patching these old bodies up so we can enjoy this life a little longer. Perhaps it is the fact we have not stressed this enough that has caused a pause in the ministry of healing.

Who Do Men Say That I AM?

The Father does these works through us, and He speaks to us and through us, just like He did with Jesus. The reason and the purpose are simple. All the glory belongs to Him. Jesus knew that. I know that. There was no way I was going to lay my hands on that woman and get her healed (if that was possible) and have her leave without Jesus in her heart and have her tell people that I healed her. This is not about us!

Perhaps you wonder what gave me the right or the authority to deal with this lady like I did. Well, according to the words spoken by Jesus, we have this kind of authority and this level of responsibility.

> *Behold, I give unto you power to tread on serpents and scorpions, and over all the power of the enemy: and nothing shall by any means hurt you.*
> *(Luke 10:19)*

I have mentioned the words power, authority, and responsibility. That is because all of these go together. They must not be separated, yet so often they have been. Consider this same verse in the Gospel of Luke from another translation.

> *Behold, I have given you authority to tread on serpents and scorpions, and over all the power of the enemy, and nothing shall hurt you.*
> *(Luke 10:19 – ESV)*

It is correct to also translate the Greek word for power as authority.[14] *Thayer's Greek Lexicon* says: "This is physical and mental power; the ability or strength with which one is endued, which he either possesses or exercises." Jesus gave us this power. He gave us this authority, and we should use it responsibly.

With all of that said, what should we conclude from these words: *but the Father that dwelleth in me, he doeth the works?* I believe the answer is both simple and obvious. Jesus was careful to give His Father all the glory for what happened. When we do the same and give recognition to the Father as Jesus did, we acknowledge our close relationship with our Heavenly Father.

This is something He will find very pleasing. But we are also making it clear we know we can never do these things without His help and guidance.

Many people have desired to be known for being able to do the things Jesus did. This does not mean they wanted to know Jesus. They wanted His fame. But they did not have the relationship I am pointing out. What was important to Jesus was not important to them. And this was obvious by their lack of character. Jesus addressed this issue one day with these remarks.

> *Not everyone that saith unto me, Lord, Lord, shall enter into the kingdom of heaven; but he that doeth the will of my Father which is in heaven. Many will say to me in that day, Lord, Lord, have we not prophesied in thy name? and in thy name have cast*

> *out devils? and in thy name done many wonderful works? And then will I profess unto them, I never knew you: depart from me, ye that work iniquity. (Matthew 7:21-23)*

Jesus did not say that these people had prophesied and cast out devils. They may have pretended to do these things or attempted to do them. But it was not real. It was not the work of the Holy Spirit. **Jesus said they will claim that they have done these things.** A notable example of some people attempting to do this is found in the Book of Acts.

> *Now God worked unusual miracles by the hands of Paul, so that even handkerchiefs or aprons were brought from his body to the sick, and the diseases left them and the evil spirits went out of them. Then some of the itinerant Jewish exorcists took it upon themselves to call the name of the Lord Jesus over those who had evil spirits, saying, "We exorcise you by the Jesus whom Paul preaches." Also there were seven sons of Sceva, a Jewish chief priest, who did so. And the evil spirit answered and said, "Jesus I know, and Paul I know; but who are you?" Then the man in whom the evil spirit was leaped on them, overpowered them, and prevailed against them, so that they fled out of that house naked and wounded. (Acts 19:11-16 – NKJV)*

These men were trying to do the works of Jesus, but they had no relationship with Jesus. Isn't it interesting that the evil spirits knew this? I can assure you that if the evil spirits knew, Jesus did too.

Doing the works of Jesus encompasses much more than working miracles, healing the sick, and casting out devils. The most important part is a close relationship with the Father. There is nothing Jesus wants for you more than for you to know His Father like He knows Him. You can have that kind of relationship. On one occasion, Jesus said this about His Father.

> *In that day you will ask in My name, and I do not say to you that I shall pray the Father for you; for the Father Himself loves you, because you have loved Me, and have believed that I came forth from God. (John 16:26-27 – NKJV)*

For Jesus to say that He *came forth from God* was not sufficient to convince many of those who followed Jesus. Some of those who followed Him were not there for the right reasons. They came looking for some flaw or a statement they could twist and use against Him. Eventually, they heard things they thought they could use to stop Him.

A group of Jews picked up rocks one day, and they were going to stone Jesus. They fully intended to kill Him if they could have. I know that sounds barbaric, but this is the attitude Jesus often faced. Jesus asked these people a question, which may have caught them off guard. Jesus wanted to know why they were about to kill Him. His words were these.

> *Many good works have I shewed you from my Father; for which of those works do ye stone me? (John 10:32)*

You may see this question as proof that all the power to do signs, wonders, healings, and miracles came from God the Father and not from Jesus. This was not the case. Jesus had this power.

> *For this purpose, the Son of God was manifested, that he might destroy the works of the devil. (1 John 3:8)*

> *The word which God sent unto the children of Israel, preaching peace by Jesus Christ: (he is Lord of all:) That word, I say, ye know, which was published throughout all Judaea, and began from Galilee, after the baptism which John preached; How God anointed Jesus of Nazareth with the Holy Ghost and with power: who went about doing good, and healing all that were oppressed of the devil; for God was with him. (Acts 10:36-38)*

John has declared that the purpose for which Jesus came to this earth was to destroy the works of the devil. John was careful to say that this was the reason the Son of God was manifested. Once again, by the wording, it can appear that the ability Jesus had to destroy the works of the devil came from the fact He was the Son of God. This would be an appropriate conclusion if we had no other verses to use for clarification.

The Greek word which has been translated as manifested[15] is a word that means to become visible or known.

Consider what that must mean in the light of our discussion. Jesus was the Son of God. But for Jesus to destroy the works of the devil, it was necessary for Him to be made visible as the Son of man. However, to do the job, Jesus needed much more than was available to Him as a mere man.

When Luke wrote the book of Acts, he agreed with this conclusion regarding the purpose for which Jesus came to earth. But Luke not only agreed with John, he went further and by using the words from a message preached by Peter in the house of Cornelius, Luke confirmed that Jesus fulfilled His purpose.

Perhaps you noticed that Luke said that God anointed Jesus with the Holy Ghost. This is not a common way of looking at the life and ministry of Jesus. Yet, there it is in print for everyone to see.

How God anointed Jesus of Nazareth with the Holy Ghost and with power. (Acts 10:38)

I want to give you something to think about that may not have previously occurred to you. Jesus was filled with the Holy Ghost.

And Jesus, full of the Holy Spirit, returned from the Jordan and was led by the Spirit in the wilderness

> *for forty days, being tempted by the devil. And he ate nothing during those days. And when they were ended, he was hungry. (Luke 4:1-2 – ESV)*

These words introduce the story of Jesus being tempted in the wilderness. I will not be discussing that story in this book. A very thorough study of this event can be found in my previous book on the life of Jesus. My purpose for including these verses is to show you that the Bible says Jesus was *full of the Holy Spirit*.

It seems very logical to think that Jesus was filled with the Holy Spirit for the same reason we are filled with the Holy Spirit. I think some people confuse **the evidence** of this infilling of the Holy Spirit with **the purpose** of this infilling. The evidence is speaking in tongues, but that is not the purpose.

The purpose for being filled with the Holy Spirit is the power we receive when we are filled. Jesus addressed this in these words.

> *But you will receive power when the Holy Spirit has come upon you, and you will be my witnesses in Jerusalem and in all Judea and Samaria, and to the end of the earth." (Acts 1:8 – ESV)*

It is noticeably clear in the statements made by Peter in the house of Cornelius that Jesus had the Holy Spirit and He had the power. This is the secret to how Jesus did the works we have heard so much about. This is the secret His imitators did not know. This is the power they were lacking.

It is possible for masses of people to be fooled. Deception is an extremely dangerous tool, and the devil uses it very effectively. If there was no other reason to know the Word of God and have a close relationship with Jesus, avoiding deception would be reason enough.

Always be wary of the mob-type excitement at huge meetings. This does not mean they are wrong. Wonderful things may be happening. But always listen carefully to what is being said. The words are more important than the activity. Pay close attention to what is said and the attitude of the people toward those on the platform. If there is not a total recognition of the Lordship of Jesus, giving all the glory to Him, it may be time to leave.

We have the same power and authority available to us that Jesus used. The same Holy Ghost and this same power make it possible for us to do the works that Jesus did. Never allow your family and friends to convince you otherwise.

The imitators are still very active. But if you learn to listen, the Holy Spirit will warn you, and you will not be deceived.

Chapter 9
His Family

Throughout the Gospel record, there are numerous places where the writers indicate that certain people had a close relationship with Jesus. It may surprise you to know that, for the most part, these were not members of "His Family." I will explain that momentarily. Then, we will also take a look at "His Close Friends."

Anyone familiar with the New Testament would surely know that one of these close friends was a young man named Lazarus, whom Jesus raised from the dead. This man had two sisters who were close friends as well. I will share some things about them. But first, it is important to examine the relationship Jesus had with His earthly family.

My goal is not just to talk about "His Family" as we know about them from the Nativity scene. Those are things we already know. I want to discover what was behind these relationships. Families have secrets, and this family did too.

If you have never been in the ministry, then you may not fully understand that the relationships a minister maintains can either help to make his or her ministry a success or it can cause their ministry to fail. Of course, there are those relationships where this would be obvious. Those are not the ones I am speaking of in this context. I am considering those which seem to be normal and acceptable, yet they wield an influence that can thwart the power of the Holy Spirit.

This was certainly true in the ministry of Jesus.

I know of no easier-to-understand example of what I just stated than the story of Jesus and His earthly family. Let's consider some of the things Jesus said, but we should also pay attention to what others said about these relationships. A good place to begin is the story of Jesus returning to His hometown after He had experienced the encounter with the devil in the wilderness.

> *And it came to pass, that when Jesus had finished these parables, he departed thence. And when he was come into his own country, he taught them in their synagogue, insomuch that they were astonished, and said, Whence hath this man this wisdom, and these mighty works? Is not this the carpenter's son? Is not his mother called Mary? and his brethren, James, and Joses, and Simon, and Judas? And his sisters, are they not all with us? Whence then hath this man all these things? And*

they were offended in him. But Jesus said unto them, A prophet is not without honor, save in his own country, and in his own house. And he did not many mighty works there because of their unbelief. (Matthew 13:53-58)

There are two versions of this story. In this version, the last statement leaves the impression that Jesus decided not to do any mighty works in His hometown. We might draw that conclusion if we only had this version of the story. This would be incorrect and unfortunate. It would appear as though Jesus was acting out of spite or even that He had been offended.

When we examine the other version of the story, it will be clear why I am willing to be so adamant about this. However, I first want to point out a few other things in this version of the story about Jesus and "His Family" and childhood friends.

Jesus went to the local Synagogue specifically to teach the people who came to the Synagogue on that day. His teaching was so profound that the people were astonished. They recognized His wisdom. They knew the stories of the mighty works He had done. We have not been afforded access to the transcript of what Jesus said, but He may have been telling them stories of the works of His Father.

What I find remarkable is the reaction of the crowd. They knew who Jesus was. They knew His mother's name and the names of His brothers.

Then the crowd stated that even His sisters were with them. If you know anything about the Jewish culture of that time, then you are aware that men were often mentioned, but as a whole women were not mentioned. The recognition Jesus gave to women in His ministry was very uncommon.

The way this part of the story ends is very strange. On the other hand, it shows a display of arrogance that is more than astounding.

They were offended[16] in him.

Because of the remarkable significance of this statement, I have set it apart and noted the meaning of the Greek word for offended. I encourage you to carefully read what the *Strong's Concordance* states in the second definition of this word. You will notice that *Thayer's Greek Lexicon*, which appears below the list of the different ways this Greek word is used in the New Testament, indicates that this is the proper way to define this word. **This crowd chose not to trust someone they should have trusted.**

It is only natural to assume that they should have trusted Him with all that Jesus had done and all the mighty miracles He had already performed. They did not. People do not trust you just because you can do miraculous things. They should have trusted Him. With all the wisdom they had received from Him, they should have trusted Him. They did not. Knowing "His Family" and their character, they should have trusted Him. They did not. And Jesus knew it.

His Family

At this point, you may already be wondering why they did not trust Jesus. I have known Jesus for over 75 years, and I don't understand why everyone does not trust Jesus. For now, let me just say it all comes back to the matter of relationships. Either the relationship is there, or it is not.

It seems obvious that Jesus could hear what they were saying about Him. He reacted to their negativity. It is found in these words.

But Jesus said unto them, A prophet is not without honor, save in his own country, and in his own house.

Jesus joined their conversation but did not react as they might have anticipated. He did not back down. Their criticism seemed to make Him bolder. He even went so far as to refer to Himself as a Prophet. We know that Jesus was a Prophet, but this crowd did not think so. I am convinced this could be a part of the same story we have another part of in the Gospel of Luke.

And he came to Nazareth, where he had been brought up: and, as his custom was, he went into the synagogue on the sabbath day, and stood up for to read. And there was delivered unto him the book of the prophet Esaias. And when he had opened the book, he found the place where it was written, The Spirit of the Lord is upon me, because he hath anointed me to preach the gospel to the poor; he hath sent me to heal the brokenhearted, to preach

*deliverance to the captives, and recovering of sight to the blind, to set at liberty them that are bruised, To preach the acceptable year of the Lord. And he closed the book, and he gave it again to the minister, and sat down. And the eyes of all them that were in the synagogue were fastened on him. And he began to say unto them, This day is this scripture fulfilled in your ears. And all bare him witness, and wondered at the gracious words which proceeded out of his mouth. And they said, Is not this Joseph's son? And he said unto them, Ye will surely say unto me this proverb, Physician, heal thyself: whatsoever we have heard done in Capernaum, do also here in thy country. And he said, Verily I say unto you, No prophet is accepted in his own country. But I tell you of a truth, many widows were in Israel in the days of Elias, when the heaven was shut up three years and six months, when great famine was throughout all the land; But unto none of them was Elias sent, save unto Sarepta, a city of Sidon, unto a woman that was a widow. And many lepers were in Israel in the time of Eliseus the prophet; and none of them was cleansed, saving Naaman the Syrian. And all they in the synagogue, when they heard these things, were filled with wrath, And rose up, and thrust him out of the city, and led him unto the brow of the hill whereon their city was built, that they might cast him down headlong. But he passing through the midst of them went his way.
(Luke 4:16-30)*

Talk about not being accepted in His own country; they tried to kill Him. When we combine this part of the story with what Matthew and Mark give us, we find something far more significant than their disrespect for Jesus.

I want to draw our attention again to these words from the book of Matthew. *And he did not many mighty works there because of their unbelief.* Relying on my years of experience in dealing with unbelief, I believe the account given by Mark is more precise. Some sources agree with me, and some do not. These are Mark's words.

> *Then He went out from there and came to His own country, and His disciples followed Him. And when the Sabbath had come, He began to teach in the synagogue. And many hearing Him were astonished, saying "Where did this Man get these things? And what wisdom is this which is given to Him, that such mighty works are performed by His hands! Is this not the carpenter, the Son of Mary, and brother of James, Joses, Judas, and Simon? And are not His sisters here with us?" So they were offended at Him. But Jesus said to them, "A prophet is not without honor except in his own country, among his own relatives, and in his own house." Now, He could do no mighty work there, except that He laid His hands on a few sick people and healed them. And He marveled because of their unbelief. Then He went about the villages in a circuit, teaching. (Mark 6:1-6 – NKJV)*

My comment about Mark being more precise is based on the difference in the story's conclusion. Matthew simply stated that Jesus **did not** do many mighty works there because of their unbelief. As I stated, this makes it appear that Jesus decided not to do any mighty works. On the other hand, Mark has declared that Jesus *could do no mighty work there, except that He laid His hands on a few sick people and healed them. And He marveled because of their unbelief.*

To say that Jesus did not do many mighty works in His hometown would imply that the issue was with Jesus. However, when the statement is made that Jesus *could do no mighty work,* we are much more inclined to ask why this was the case. **Choosing not to do something** is vastly different from **being unable to do something**. The answer is given in the next statement.

It was because of their unbelief.

Yes, the unbelief of the people in Jesus' hometown stopped the miraculous. As strange as that might sound, it is true. I know this flies in the face of the doctrine of the sovereignty of God. Those who hold to a very rigid notion of God's sovereignty want to believe God can do anything He pleases anytime He wants to. The fact of the matter is that God has so structured his relationship with man that He has limited what He can do. In this case, unbelief is the limitation.

Jesus could not do just anything He wanted to do anytime He desired to do it. He was anointed by the Holy

His Family

Ghost, and it still was not true. For that matter, unbelief is blocking a lot of what God wants to do today. I have witnessed it many times during the years I have been in the ministry.

My wife Donna and I moved to Tulsa, Oklahoma, many years ago. We were asked to make the move by a large ministry located in this city. I had been hired to be the dean of the school that this ministry had established. Not long after we moved to Tulsa, I spoke in one of the local churches.

Before the service began that Sunday night, my wife was seated close to the front of the auditorium, directly behind the wife of the pastor of this church. The lady did not know my wife, and she did not know me. Another lady seated close by engaged the pastor's wife in conversation and asked her if she knew who would speak that night. The pastor's wife said: "I don't know him, but I have heard he is not any good."

I did not know about the conversation my wife had overheard until after the service. But when I got up to speak, I had my wife stand, and I introduced her to the church audience. The pastor's wife turned around and saw my wife was seated right behind her. Donna had overheard this lady's remark. Did the pastor's wife apologize? No.

In that service, I had no unction to pray for the sick. I was eager to get through my message and leave and I never wanted to preach there again. It seemed that no one in the audience was paying any attention to what I said. I did not know why until after I heard this story from my wife.

I am glad I did not have any direction in that service to minister personally to the people. It would have been almost impossible to have any results. This attitude of disrespect for other ministers had permeated this congregation. It does not matter how young and inexperienced a man or woman of God may be; they should be respected as gifts from God. This respect for ministers is crucial for the health and unity of the church. About 25 years later, I was invited to speak in the same church. They had changed pastors, but that same unteachable spirit and dishonor were prevalent in that congregation. In fact, it had gotten much worse.

Lest you think this is only about disrespect, let's consider the matter of what this disrespect creates. In the Gospels of Matthew and Mark, it is called unbelief.[17] This word means a great deal more than meets the eye.

Should you choose to look this word up, you will find that after the remarks from *Strong*, toward the bottom of the page, *Thayer* identifies this word as meaning something that is "shown in withholding belief in the divine power - or in the power and promises of God by opposition to the Gospel - with the added notion of obstinacy."

Please note that I have pieced this definition together without including the Biblical references where this same Greek word is used. I have only done this because it gets us closer to understanding what Jesus was facing in the town where He grew up. *Thayer* has illustrated the various aspects of the word as it is used in different Scriptures. I have provided this view of the word unbelief to show that in each case, the people involved made a choice not to believe.

This is precisely what the people in Nazareth did. They were not just in doubt of the ability of Jesus to do mighty works. There was proof He could do them. He had already done wonderful things for those who believed in Him. There was no doubt that He could heal the sick and perform miracles.

This crowd decided not to believe Jesus could do these things in Nazareth.

They had decided not to believe Jesus could do anything for them. **Can you see why Jesus could not have a close relationship with His brothers after His ministry began?** If, in just one meeting, their unbelief succeeded in stopping Jesus from doing miracles and restricted Him to only healing a few sick folks, what would have happened to His ministry if they had been with Him all the time? The stories we have in the Gospels would not exist. The very reasons Jesus came to earth would have been stymied.

Decisions like this are still being made today. Churches are filled with people who have embraced unbelief. The Pastor's wife I spoke of earlier, whom I had never met, had already decided I had nothing to say that would benefit her or their church. But many pastors want people like these in attendance because their presence increases the size of the church and some of them give a lot of money. The cost of unbelief is extremely high. It not only hinders the work of Jesus but also affects the church and its members in profound ways. No church can afford it.

But there is more that I should say about the earthly family of the Lord Jesus. Mary, the mother of Jesus, believed in Him. That much is clear, and thank God she did. Mary provoked Jesus to perform His first miracle and turn water into wine. That shows an absence of unbelief in her life. Of course, by this time, Jesus had collected a group of men around Him who believed in Him sufficiently to do what He asked them to do. And this brings me to another important part of this story. What is the real significance of all of this?

I am attempting to show that if we are going to be used by God in doing the works that Jesus did, there will be relationships we must avoid. And in some cases, that means members of our immediate family. Perhaps a word of caution is in order. What I am writing in this chapter is not something that is well understood. Some people find this very offensive. Yet this is what Jesus said about it.

> *And every one that hath forsaken houses, or brethren, or sisters, or father, or mother, or wife, or children, or lands, for my name's sake, shall receive a hundredfold and shall inherit everlasting life. (Matthew 19:29)*

It is not so much a matter of Jesus asking us to leave these people and these things. He may and He may not. It is

His Family

a fact that Jesus recognized that often, we have no choice if we are going to follow Him and do what He has asked us to do for Him.

We do not travel on a higher plane than the one our Lord walked. Thank God the issues I have written about are not a factor in every family, but it is true in many. It is commonly accepted among Biblical scholars that none of the members of the immediate family of Jesus became his disciples. I am speaking of the twelve men Jesus chose at the beginning of His ministry.

There appears to be enough evidence to say that two of the twelve men Jesus chose were His cousins. It is commonly held that Mary, the mother of Jesus, was the sister of a lady named Salome. This lady had two sons who became disciples of Jesus. This means that two of the twelve disciples were His cousins. These two men were James and John, who are also referred to as the sons of Zebedee.

Some scholars are willing to stretch things a little and suggest that some of the other disciples may have also been relatives. Whether or not this is true, we can't be absolutely certain. It is striking that Jesus did not choose members of His immediate family. I think the story we have examined tells us why this is the case.

It makes me wonder what His brothers and sisters thought when Jesus appeared to them after the resurrection. No, I don't have any Scripture to base this on other than the fact that Jesus loved them. We know Jesus made His identity known to many people during those forty days. I suspect that Jesus used this opportunity to overwhelm the unbelief in those He loved so much. This is the first thing He did with Peter and Thomas. Why wouldn't He go to His family and His friends and do the same?

Chapter 10
His Close Friends

As informative as it is to think about the people Jesus did not have a close relationship with during His ministry, it is even more helpful to think about those friends to which He was close. There appears to have been several people who were close friends with Jesus. Some are only mentioned, and yet, with others, we have been provided considerable insight.

The first three people that come to mind are Lazarus, Mary, and Martha. Consider this passage as I use it to explain my conclusions. (You will probably notice that because this is a lengthy passage, I have removed the details about the miracle that Jesus performed.) I want to focus all of your attention on this very close friendship.

> *Now a certain man was sick, Lazarus of Bethany, the town of Mary and her sister Martha. It was that Mary who anointed the Lord with fragrant oil and wiped His feet with her hair, whose brother*

Lazarus was sick. Therefore, the sisters sent to Him, saying, "Lord, behold, he whom You love is sick." When Jesus heard that, He said, "This sickness is not unto death, but for the glory of God, that the Son of God may be glorified through it." Now Jesus loved Martha and her sister and Lazarus. So, when He heard that he was sick, He stayed two more days in the place where He was. Then after this He said to the disciples, "Let us go to Judea again." The disciples said to Him, "Rabbi, lately the Jews sought to stone You, and are You going there again?" Jesus answered, "Are there not twelve hours in the day? If anyone walks in the day, he does not stumble, because he sees the light of this world. But if one walks in the night, he stumbles, because the light is not in him." These things He said, and after that He said to them, "Our friend Lazarus sleeps, but I go that I may wake him up." Then His disciples said, "Lord, if he sleeps he will get well." However, Jesus spoke of his death, but they thought that He was speaking about taking rest in sleep. Then Jesus said to them plainly, "Lazarus is dead Then Thomas, who is called the Twin, said to his fellow disciples, "Let us also go, that we may die with Him." Then Martha, as soon as she heard that Jesus was coming, went and met Him, but Mary was sitting in the house. Now Martha said to Jesus, "Lord, if You had been here, my brother would not have died. But even now I know that whatever You ask of God, God will give You." She said to Him,

"Yes, Lord, I believe that You are the Christ, the Son of God, who is to come into the world." And when she had said these things, she went her way and secretly called Mary her sister, saying, "The Teacher has come and is calling for you." As soon as she heard that, she arose quickly and came to Him Then, when Mary came where Jesus was, and saw Him, she fell down at His feet, saying to Him, "Lord, if You had been here, my brother would not have died." Therefore, when Jesus saw her weeping, and the Jews who came with her weeping, He groaned in the spirit and was troubled. And He said, "Where have you laid him?" They said to Him, "Lord, come and see." Jesus wept. Then the Jews said, "See how He loved him!"
(John 11:1-36 – NKJV)

The first thing to take note of in this story is that John explained that this Mary was the same lady who had previously taken an expensive bottle of fragrant oil and used it to anoint the feet of Jesus. She had then wiped the feet of Jesus with her hair. This story is recorded in John Chapter 12.

However, I think John mentioned this in the context of the story about the death of Lazarus as a way of emphasizing how close this lady was to Jesus. The fragrant oil was something most people could not afford. And they certainly would not pour it on the feet of a casual acquaintance. These three people were remarkably close to Jesus. This Mary and another woman whose name we are not given are the only people we know about whoever made such a public and costly display of their love and adoration of Jesus.

Mary and her sister Martha had very different ways of expressing their love for the Lord. For Mary, it was to sit at His feet and listen and learn from Him. For Martha, it was to fix a favorite meal and serve it to Jesus. Both are noteworthy; however, Jesus made a point regarding which one was more important. Luke brings all of this out very clearly.

> *But Martha was cumbered about much serving, and came to him, and said, Lord, dost thou not care that my sister hath left me to serve alone? bid her therefore that she help me. And Jesus answered and said unto her, Martha, Martha, thou art careful and troubled about many things: But one thing is needful: and Mary hath chosen that good part, which shall not be taken away from her.*
> *(Luke 10:40-42)*

The New Living Translation provides a better expression of what Jesus said to Martha. When Jesus said: *Martha, Martha, thou art careful and troubled about many things: But one thing is needful:* I don't see this so much as a rebuke as I do an effort on the part of Jesus to make sure Martha knew He appreciated what she was doing for Him. However, He also wanted Martha to discover the depth of the relationship Mary had with Him. She needed to know there was something else that was more important. Jesus desired that same type of relationship with Martha.

Solid relationships are not built on the foundation of rebukes. It is understanding between two people that will cause a relationship to grow. Just because one priority is more important than another, it does not necessarily mean we should completely eliminate the lower priority. The best approach is to adjust the priorities. I believe this is what Jesus wanted Martha to understand.

> *But Martha was distracted by the big dinner she was preparing. She came to Jesus and said, "Lord, doesn't it seem unfair to you that my sister just sits here while I do all the work? Tell her to come and help me." But the Lord said to her, "My dear Martha, you are worried and upset over all these details! There is only one thing worth being concerned about. Mary has discovered it, and it will not be taken away from her."*
> (Luke 10:40-42 – NLT)

Martha raised the issue of fairness. But did you notice that Jesus completely ignored that remark? Jesus knew the real problem. It was clear to Jesus that Martha did not understand the significance of what Mary had discovered in her relationship with Him. This is much more common than you might think.

There have been many occasions over the years when kind and loving people have endeavored to help me with what I was doing in the ministry. There was no doubt in my mind that they meant well. They wanted to help, and I did appreciate their efforts. But for some reason, they did not notice what I thought was most important. At times it can seem as though this strong desire to be helpful is not only misguided, but it may have an ulterior motive. It is always important not to prejudge the motives of another person.

Jesus read this situation perfectly. It is important for leadership to learn to do the same. When dealing with touchy situations, it has been my experience that the best approach is to focus more on attitudes than words.

It is always possible to be surrounded by wonderful people who love you and want to do anything they can to serve you. This was Martha. But the people who are needed the most are those who have the same vision as the minister. Then, they need to have the same commitment to see the vision fulfilled. For these reasons, John begins his story of the death and resurrection of Lazarus as he does.

John made the statement in the Gospel he gave us that there was a specific reason for his writing. I certainly do not claim my books to be on the same level as the Gospel of John, but my purpose is the same.

> John said: *And truly Jesus did many other signs in the presence of His disciples, which are not written in this book; but these are written that you may believe that Jesus is the Christ, the Son of God, and that believing you may have life in His name.*
> (John 20:30-31 – NKJV)

His Close Friends

These things are written that you may believe. John had observed the elevated level of unbelief that Jesus encountered. Yet, John knew that Jesus was the Christ. He embraced the fact that Jesus was the Son of God, and he wanted others to do the same. I wholeheartedly agree. This is the path to having life in His name. And I do not just speak of eternal life, even though that is the most important thing. Many things have been robbed from the body of Christ because of unbelief.

We have a life to pursue during the years we spend on earth. A great deal of this life is to be spent in preparation for the life to come. But we must never forget that God desires for us to enjoy this life. The devil must be very aware of this. I base that on the fact that the devil is constantly attempting to steal, destroy, and even kill those who love Jesus. Knowing this certainly means we have no time to allow for unbelief. Never open that door in your life.

Jesus found this to be critical and guarded His relationships accordingly. I am endeavoring to do the same. Jesus had a zero-tolerance policy when it came to unbelief. He did not hang around people who thought and acted in that way. You can never build a good relationship with someone who does not believe in you. It should be clear that the secret here is our relationships. It should also be clear that if people do not believe in you, then you will not believe in them either.

The next statement from John is a clear indication from Mary and Martha concerning the relationship Jesus had with Lazarus. *Therefore, the sisters sent to Him, saying, "Lord, behold, he whom You love is sick."* After making His statement that God would be glorified through the sickness that came on Lazarus, we are given this assessment of the relationship. *Now Jesus loved Martha and her sister and Lazarus.* This was common knowledge. It seems clear that Jesus spent a lot of time with these three people, even staying in their home.

I find it interesting that John did not say that Jesus loved Mary and her sister. It makes me wonder if the love between Jesus and Mary was so obvious that it did not need to be mentioned. But perhaps John was prompted by the Holy Spirit to also make it clear that Jesus loved Martha.

It is common for all of us to put the spotlight on the people for whom we have an obvious affinity. Maybe we need to take a lesson from John and be clearer that we also deeply appreciate the others in our life that we tend to rarely ever mention. I will repeat the context of our study and add a few more comments.

> *As Jesus and the disciples continued on their way to Jerusalem, they came to a certain village where a woman named Martha welcomed him into her home. Her sister, Mary, sat at the Lord's feet, listening to what he taught. But Martha was distracted by the big dinner she was preparing. She came to Jesus and said, "Lord, doesn't it seem unfair to you that my sister just sits here while I do all the work? Tell her to come and help me."*
> *(Luke 10:38-40 – NLT)*

His Close Friends

Knowing all these things makes it seem odd that Jesus would delay His trip to their home when He learned that Lazarus was sick. I want to be truly clear that the sickness that caused Lazarus to die did not bring glory to God. What brought the glory was the response Jesus made after the sickness had caused Lazarus to die.

Jesus knew that Lazarus was going to die. Jesus also knew that He could and that He would raise Lazarus from the dead. I should mention that if you intend to raise a person from the dead and you have any questions about your ability to do it, you would be better off leaving them alone.

Jesus had to know how sad the death of their brother was going to make both Mary and Martha. It made Jesus sad. In this story, we find one of the best-known Scriptures about Jesus.

When Jesus went to see this family and found out that they had buried Lazarus, we are told that Mary and some others were weeping. Then, we have the shortest verse in the Bible. *Jesus wept.*

However, Jesus did not stop with the tears. Too many people stop with the tears. He shed tears all right, and I believe it was because He shared the pain and anguish that Mary and Martha were experiencing. But Jesus moved on from the tears to the solution. It was at this point that Jesus requested to know the location where they had buried Lazarus. And as you know, Jesus raised him from the dead.

This should cause us to wonder why Jesus was able to do such a marvelous thing for this family yet not be able to do anything for His own family. It was the matter of where Jesus found faith and where He encountered unbelief. This brings us back to the Gospel of John.

First, I will draw your attention to the remarks made by the disciples when Jesus told them they would visit Mary, Martha, and Lazarus. Some of the disciples said: *"Rabbi, lately the Jews sought to stone You, and are You going there again?"* They knew that Jesus loved Lazarus. But simultaneously, they questioned the wisdom of Jesus risking His own life to see His friend. Jesus was more than willing to take that risk.

The disciples did not understand why Jesus had come to earth. He was always willing to die for those He loved.

Once Thomas knew Jesus was determined to make the trip to Bethany, *Then Thomas, who is called the Twin, said to his fellow disciples, "Let us also go, that we may die with Him."* I would call that an expression of sarcastic love.

Thomas cared enough about Jesus to make the trip through this dangerous territory with Him and even die protecting Him if that became necessary. But Thomas did not have enough faith in Jesus to accept that this trip was a good idea. He questioned the wisdom of Jesus, and he questioned the ability of Jesus to keep them safe. Interestingly enough, Thomas did not seem to have a problem with what Jesus might do for his dead friend once He got to Bethany.

Jesus knew Thomas was like this when He chose him to be one of His disciples. **It is not possible to only be surrounded by people who all have their act together.** We are all growing. We are all learning. Some things we know and believe, and other things we just don't know enough to believe. Never forget it is love that binds us together. It is not that we are so smart or that we have everything figured out.

The Holy Ghost was constantly leading Jesus and teaching Jesus as a man. Jesus listened very carefully to the words His Father spoke to Him. He obeyed His Father no matter what His friends and His family may have thought of Him. These human relationships were particularly important to Him. Yet there was never a more important relationship to Jesus than the one He had with His Father.

There is one more close human relationship that Jesus had that I would like to consider. It is the relationship Jesus had with Mary Magdalene. This was a very different Mary. There are six women mentioned in the New Testament who were called Mary.

The Bible says that Mary Magdalene was demon-possessed when she met Jesus. We know that part to be a fact because Jesus cast seven demons out of her. However, despite what has become a popular opinion, the Bible never says that Mary was a prostitute. I know that is a popular opinion, but it is not true. This is an assumption that some have made because of their interpretation of certain passages and the way they link the stories together. Here is the Biblical record.

> *Now it came to pass, afterward, that He went through every city and village, preaching and bringing the glad tidings of the kingdom of God. And the twelve were with Him, and certain women who had been healed of evil spirits and infirmities, Mary called Magdalene, out of whom had come seven demons, and Joanna the wife of Chuza, Herod's steward, and Susanna, and many others who provided for Him with their substance.*
> *(Luke 8:1-2 – NKJV)*

Another point of confusion about Mary Magdalene is that she is the woman mentioned in this next story, which I have taken from the Gospel of Luke. Please notice that Luke never mentions this woman's name.

> *Then one of the Pharisees asked Him to eat with him. And He went to the Pharisee's house, and sat down to eat. And behold, a woman in the city who was a sinner, when she knew that Jesus sat at the table in the Pharisee's house, brought an alabaster flask of fragrant oil, and stood at His feet behind Him weeping; and she began to wash His feet with her tears, and wiped them with the hair of her head; and she kissed His feet and anointed them with the fragrant oil.*
> *(Luke 7:36-38 – NKJV)*

This story is sometimes confused with the one about Mary, the brother of Lazarus. The difference between the two stories should be obvious, but it must not be. In his Gospel, John is careful to draw attention to the fact that the Mary he was about to mention was the sister of Lazarus. John seems to want those who read his book to know that this Mary anointed the feet of Jesus with a pound of spikenard. I am sure John knew about this and other similar events. Also, Mary, the sister of Lazarus, is never referred to as a sinner, or a woman in the city, or a person who had demons cast out of her.

The woman mentioned in the Gospel of Luke was known as *a woman in the city,* and she was also called *a sinner.* While these bits of information do set this woman apart from other women, she was not called a prostitute. As I stated previously, that is the common opinion. She anointed the feet of Jesus with a precious ointment from an alabaster (flask) or box. Nothing is said in Luke chapter 7 about Jesus casting demons out of her.

It is easy to see why a person could draw this terribly negative opinion of this woman. To call her *a woman in the city* means something. Combine that with the word *sinner,* and it starts to be easy to think of this woman negatively. She was deeply moved to be standing in the presence of Jesus. The fact that she had the money to purchase something like this alabaster box of fragrant oil makes her seem even more suspicious. It is in this context that we often see the nature of Jesus. When others quickly looked for reasons to condemn, Jesus looked for reasons to love and forgive. Regardless of our background and the life we may have lived, we should all be grateful for His love and forgiving spirit.

The primary similarity in those stories is the matter of two different women washing the feet of Jesus with fragrant oil and wiping His feet with their hair. The container for this pound of spikenard, which is a juice from an East Indian plant, is never mentioned. Yet we are told the fragrant oil was contained in an alabaster[18] box. It is commonly believed this was probably myrrh.[19]

I am sure you can tell I do not think this was Mary, the sister of Lazarus, who was a woman from the city. Mary, the sister of Lazarus, is spoken of in terms of respect. Neither do I find it necessary to think this was Mary Magdalene. Mary Magdalene had her issues, but not every demon-possessed woman is a prostitute.

It is the statement made by Jesus about His burial that some have used to say this woman mentioned in Luke 7 and in John 12 is the same person. Myrrh was one of the ointments used by Joseph and Nicodemus to prepare the body of Jesus for burial. Mary Magdalene, being the first person at the tomb on the day Jesus rose from the dead, does not automatically tie her to the possession of myrrh.

We have this marvelous story of Mary Magdalene at the tomb of Jesus right after the resurrection. It was still dark when she arrived and found the tomb empty. And then the most amazing thing happened. Mary Magdalene was the first person Jesus made Himself known to after the resurrection. This Mary was there at the tomb because of a heart of gratitude and love. Few of His friends loved Him like this woman. Few of them were eager to see if what Jesus had told them was true. This Mary may not have expected to meet the resurrected Jesus, but neither did anyone else. So, why sully the story of this woman by calling her a prostitute?

What are we to make of all of this? While we can't prove exactly which Mary is which, after all, there are six different Marys mentioned in the New Testament, we do have evidence of this.

Jesus is not looking for perfect people and neither should we.

A person with a new heart committed to Jesus can make the best friend you ever have. It was the condition of the heart of the family and friends of Jesus that caused them to be filled with unbelief. Conversely, the heart condition of Mary, Martha, Lazarus, and Mary Magdalene caused them to be the people they became. They made themselves available to be the friends of Jesus.

Jesus did not encounter unbelief when He arrived at Bethany. He made sure of it. He went there because His friend had died. But when Jesus arrived, He first met Martha. *Martha said to Jesus, "Lord, if You had been here, my brother would not have died. But even now I know that whatever You ask of God, God will give You."*

We can focus on the statement that if Jesus had been there, Lazarus would not have died. Many others have done that. Martha was not the only one to say this. Mary said the same thing. However, when we look at the following verses, we can learn how Jesus assessed the situation for the possibility of unbelief. Here are the statements.

> *Jesus said to her, "Your brother will rise again." Martha answered, "I know he will rise again in the resurrection at the last day." Jesus said to her, "I am the resurrection and the life. The one who believes in me will live, even though they die; and whoever lives by believing in me will never die. Do you believe this?" "Yes, Lord," she replied, "I believe that you are the Messiah, the Son of God, who is to come into the world." (John 11:22-27 – NIV)*

Can you see that Jesus wanted to know what Martha believed? Jesus wanted to know if Martha believed what He said. Did she believe He was *the resurrection and the life?* Did Martha believe in Jesus so much that she could embrace His claim that *the one who believes in me will live, even though they die; and whoever lives by believing in me will never die?* Jesus waited for her answer.

Consider the statement Martha made before this part of the conversation. Martha had said, *"I know that whatever You ask of God, God will give You."* Let me state this another way. Martha appears to have had no faith that Jesus could raise her brother from the dead. It was not her faith that brought her brother back to life. However, there was no unbelief in Martha to prevent Jesus from raising him from the dead.

Martha was asking Jesus to do something about her brother. She wanted Jesus to do something by being there before he died. Now that he was dead, Jesus wanted her to ask Him to do something about her dead brother. Martha knew Jesus could have done something if He had arrived before Lazarus died. She even believed that if Jesus asked God to do something after Lazarus died, God would do it. She said if you ask for it, God will do it.

Jesus was challenging Martha. It seems as if He was asking her: "What if you ask for it?" "What if you ask me to raise your brother from the dead?" "Consider it, Martha." *I am the resurrection and the life.* "**Ask me.**" *The one who believes in me will live, even though they die; and whoever lives by believing in me will never die.* "Martha, you believe that if I ask God, He will do what I ask. Do you believe that **if you ask me**, I will do what you ask?" Now, take that and make it personal.

You may believe that if Oral Roberts or some other healing evangelist was still alive, they could ask God to heal someone you know, and God would hear them and do it. But what about you? What if you asked? Could you lay your hands on a sick person and expect them to get well? Would God hear and answer what you ask?

I believe that a huge problem in the body of Christ today is a problem of unbelief. Some of this is the result of claims made by people that God was going to do certain things, and they never happened. However, the greater issue may be that so many Christians believe that God will answer the prayers of some person of renown, but they don't believe He will answer their prayers.

One of my favorite passages of scripture to think about when discussing the subject of faith versus unbelief is the story told in the book of Acts about the lame man who was laid at the Beautiful Gate of the Temple every day.

While this man was not healed because of his faith but rather through the manifestation of the gifts of the Spirit, it is clear there was no unbelief in this man's heart. This is what the Bible tells us about this lame man and the miraculous intervention of the Holy Spirit in his life.

> *Now Peter and John went up together to the temple at the hour of prayer, the ninth hour. And a certain man lame from his mother's womb was carried, whom they laid daily at the gate of the temple which is called Beautiful, to ask alms from those who entered the temple; who, seeing Peter and John about to go into the temple, asked for alms. And fixing his eyes on him, with John, Peter said, "Look at us." So he gave them his attention, expecting to receive something from them. Then Peter said, "Silver and gold I do not have, but what I do have I give you: In the name of Jesus Christ of Nazareth, rise up and walk." And he took him by the right hand and lifted him up, and immediately his feet and ankle bones received strength. So he, leaping*

up, stood and walked and entered the temple with them—walking, leaping, and praising God.
(Acts 3:1-8 – NKJV)

When Peter told this man to look at them, he wanted this man to **expect to receive** something from them. Too often, we don't want people to look at us because we don't want them to expect something from us. Maybe that is because we have nothing of real, lasting value to give them, and we know it. Peter and John knew they had the God-given ability to provide precisely what this man needed. We might assume the man needed money so he could buy food. That is a reasonable assumption. However, his need for a miracle was greater than his need for money.

This is what Peter was talking about when he told the man that they had no silver or gold. I am not willing to assume that they had no money. Neither do I think these men always carried gold and silver. It makes sense to me that Peter wanted to get the attention off of what the man was begging for. No amount of money could fix this man's problem.

Most of the time, people want what they think they need, and maybe there is some reality to it. But like this man, many people have given up hope concerning their real needs. Some of this could be because there has been so much deceit and lack of honesty concerning the miraculous that many will not ask for what they need. They don't ask God for what they need, and perhaps it is because they are not sure He would give it to them.

This could be due to a lack of teaching. Or it could be due to disappointment that has built up over several years. The unbelief of a few has dealt a terrible blow to many in desperate need.

I have had many people (some with profoundly serious problems) want me to ask the Father for their miracle or their healing. They wanted me to do this on their behalf. I am glad to do it. But I would prefer that their faith grow to the point that they would have personal confidence in asking.

On occasion, we all need help. Some problems are too big for us to carry by ourselves. When we are in these situations, where do we go? Who do we look to? Who do we know that we have enough confidence in that if they made statements like Peter made, we would believe them? And if we believe them and expect things to come from God through them to us, and it does not happen, then where do we stand?

I have just described the nexus of unbelief.

Unbelief is very real, and it permeates the very atmosphere of many churches. This should not be. Jesus had dealt with this many times. Jesus was determined to get Mary and Martha beyond this point. Jesus did this often. This was a great part of the secret to His success. Jesus could move people to believe in Him.

No matter who you are, you have to believe in somebody. If you don't, then you are all alone.

If you are looking for the perfect person to believe in, you have a problem. It is a big problem. There are no perfect people. So, find someone who often does the right thing. Find someone who does get results most of the time. Find someone who has a pure heart and who wants to help. Whatever you do, don't let unbelief take up residence in your heart.

Can you see the connection between what I have just written about and the ministry of Jesus? No matter how greatly a person is anointed, that person must have the right relationships if they are going to do well in the ministry. This is not an easy task. Every minister is looking for people to believe in them. Is this wrong?

Jesus was looking for people to believe in Him. **It is not the search that is the issue. It is the reason for the search.**

Jesus wanted people to believe in Him so He could help them. He knew not all of them could become close friends. First of all, there were too many of them. But more importantly, they could not all be in a close relationship because they did not all believe in Him for the right reasons.

Jesus was looking for men and women to believe in Him so they would help Him be of help to other people. One of the worst things a minister endures is dealing with people who only want attention because of what they can get. What is needed is more people who desire to be associated with ministers because of what they can help them do and what they can help them give.

One man among those Jesus chose opened himself up to the devil. The others did not. That one lone act on the part of Judas Iscariot makes it even more remarkable. Some of these men were slow to grasp what Jesus was about. But history records that all the other eleven eventually figured out why they were privileged to have had such a close personal relationship with Jesus.

I am very blessed to have wonderful people around me. My wife is such a precious and awesome person. God blessed me with a beautiful lady I have been married to for many years. She has faithfully walked beside me every step of the way. I have two wonderful sons. One is in Heaven now. The other is still here. They have always indicated their confidence in my ability to follow the leading of the Lord, and it has taken many twists and turns. Our sons married beautiful young ladies who serve the Lord with gladness. And now we have three grandchildren who know the Lord.

I am grateful, incredibly grateful. Many who have served the Lord and done remarkable things for God could not say what I have said. Frankly, I find that to be sad. It should not be this way. But somehow, they found people who believed in them.

Maybe it is your time to step up in the life of some man or woman of God and demonstrate your love and support. Jesus needed this, and He sought it and found it. Lots of people are still waiting. So, what about you? Are you ready and willing to be a real friend of someone who is called by God?

It is too easy to think we only need the Holy Ghost. Yes, we do need Him. But remember, just as it is impossible to replace the power and influence of the Holy Ghost in our lives, it is equally impossible to do what God put us here to do without the right human relationships.

Chapter 11
His Disciples

Jesus, at the outset of His ministry, handpicked twelve men. These twelve men with different backgrounds, from diverse occupations and socioeconomic standings, would embark on a journey filled with both exhilarating experiences and arduous days alongside the Son of man. For the most part, they were in constant companionship with Jesus for about three years. The kind of men Jesus chose tells us a lot about Him.

Just for the sake of some interesting thoughts, I will raise these questions and leave them for you to answer. If Jesus was only the Son of God and did everything as God, why would He need the help of twelve men? Why bother? What did it matter what humans thought? Why not just go about His business as God and make things happen the way He wanted? How can this be reconciled with the extreme teaching on the sovereignty of God? There are obvious reasons for Jesus choosing the men He picked. But does any of this have anything to do with who Jesus was and is? I believe it does!

These twelve men played a significant role in the ministry of Jesus. This was, in fact, both good and bad. We know a great deal about some of them, and some are only briefly mentioned. However, I am certain Jesus chose each of these men for a specific reason. As far as the ministry is concerned, His choices reveal a great deal about this aspect of the work of the Holy Spirit in the ministry of Jesus. Choosing the right people to do the many things that must be done in a ministry is one of the most challenging parts of the task.

As I discuss this facet of the ministry, it's crucial to remember that the purpose of this discussion is not to devote a lot of time and space talking about these individuals. Rather, it illustrates how the Holy Spirit led Jesus to choose these men, all of whom had a destiny to fulfill in the ministry of Jesus. Their roles were of such significance that His variety of choices tells us a great deal about who Jesus is.

Those who are familiar with the story of the life of Jesus are probably already thinking of what they know about men such as Peter and Judas Iscariot. These names are well known. While they played a prominent role and are very visible in the Gospels, they are not the only ones who were extremely important to this ministry.

At the time this book is being written, I have spent over 60 years in the ministry. One thing I learned during the early days of my ministry is just how important it is to be surrounded by the right people. This is a more challenging task than it might seem because the more deeply they are involved in a leadership role of the ministry, the more crucial it is for these to be the right people. They either help you do what God has called you to do, or they hinder you. Whether you choose to believe it or not, these hindrances can, at times, become almost impossible to overcome.

In leadership, there is no room for indecision. It may sound stringent, but it is the truth. When it comes to following the direction of the Holy Spirit, it's a choice: either obey or disobey! This means those around you will either bolster your obedience and assist you, or they will do the opposite.

A series of what appears to be relatively small acts of disobedience by various church staff members can escalate to the point of a huge disaster. I have seen it happen on several occasions. If you look closely at the three years these twelve men spent with Jesus, you will see several examples of what I just said. And yes, I am calling these disciples His staff. Yet Jesus was always able to avoid the disaster. This was the work of the Holy Spirit in His ministry.

Just because we know extraordinarily little about some of the people mentioned among the twelve disciples does not mean they were unimportant and non-committal. It does not mean they were not good disciples. It does not mean they did not play a role. It does not mean they were a hindrance.

There are several places in the Bible where these disciples are mentioned. First, I want to share with you the complete list. Then, I will show you why I think this subject of the choosing of these twelve men matters so much. These choices were important both at the beginning and the end of the ministry of Jesus on this earth.

To the extent that we are provided enough information in the Bible, we will look at the moment Jesus chose each of these men. One of our goals is to discover how He made His choices. Exactly what was Jesus looking for in each of these men? This tells us as much, if not more, about Jesus and how the Holy Spirit was functioning in Him as it does about these twelve men. Choices of this magnitude say a great deal about who a person is.

Consider the possibility that when Jesus confronted His disciples about who they thought He was, something else must have been in the back of His mind. He chose these men. After spending time with them, how had He influenced them? Was it obvious to these men that Jesus had chosen them because **who they were** reflected to others vital information about Him? As someone has so aptly said, "Everything produces after its own kind." Some ministers tend to forget that.

On the following pages I have provided the list of the twelve disciples as it is recorded by Matthew, Mark, and Luke. While there are differences in some of the names, the three Gospel writers have all written about the same twelve individuals. The reason for including all three examples is the various ancillary information found in each example by these different men.

I find this interesting. It makes me wonder why they did not include more of this kind of information.

> *And when he had called unto him his twelve disciples, he gave them power against unclean spirits, to cast them out, and to heal all manner of sickness and all manner of disease. Now the names of the twelve apostles are these; The first, Simon, who is called Peter, and Andrew his brother; James the son of Zebedee, and John his brother; Philip, and Bartholomew; Thomas, and Matthew the publican; James the son of Alphaeus, and Lebbaeus, whose surname was Thaddaeus; Simon the Canaanite, and Judas Iscariot, who also betrayed him. (Matthew 10:1-4)*

Several things are immediately made clear from this passage. It is undeniable that Jesus chose all twelve of these men with the full expectation that they would do the things He gave them the power to do. This is a splendid example of who Jesus was. This is how He thought. I base this on the fact that I believe Jesus spoke with them in some detail as He chose them. I am not convinced that we have a record of everything that was said. Thus, I have these questions.

Did all twelve of these men do what Jesus empowered them to do? At best, the answer to that question is not known with any certainty. We have a few statements that imply they all followed through, but I can't help but wonder if Judas Iscariot ever laid his hands on the sick and healed them. Did

Thomas demonstrate this power over unclean spirits? There are stories that indicate Thomas did wonderful things after the Day of Pentecost.[20] We are also provided notable examples of what most of the other disciples did. What can we learn from it? Should we expect to do the same?

Family relationships were important to Jesus. But as I have stated, so was the issue of unbelief, which appears to have been strong among some of His siblings. I have mentioned the fact that none of His brothers are numbered among the twelve disciples. Yet, He did choose young men from other families. He chose men who were friends. Some of these men were in business together. Then, He chose a man that none of the others would have picked because, as you may already know, he was a tax collector.

> These verses tell us that there was *Philip and Bartholomew; Thomas and Matthew the tax collector; James son of Alphaeus, and Thaddaeus; Simon the Zealot and Judas Iscariot, who betrayed him. (Matthew 10:3-4 – NIV)*

Matthew was the tax collector. I find it interesting that Matthew is usually listed next to the man who came to be known as "doubting Thomas" because of his reaction to the news that Jesus had risen from the dead. What are we to infer from this pairing? Is it of any consequence? It may indicate how the writer felt about these two men instead of how they fared as disciples. We do find a refreshing degree of transparency in the Bible.

As if the interaction of this group of men was not going to create enough drama, Jesus also chose a Zealot. Jesus had no fear of conflict. When Jesus made His decision to choose twelve men, He knew there would be plenty of disagreement.

Mark and Luke also include a list of these twelve men. Considering those passages provides a more complete picture of this group of men.

> *He appointed twelve that they might be with him and that he might send them out to preach and to have authority to drive out demons. These are the twelve he appointed: Simon (to whom he gave the name Peter), James son of Zebedee and his brother John (to them he gave the name Boanerges, which means "sons of thunder"), Andrew, Philip, Bartholomew, Matthew, Thomas, James son of Alphaeus, Thaddaeus, Simon the Zealot and Judas Iscariot, who betrayed him.*
> *(Mark 3:14-19 – NIV)*[21]

Mark provides some of the same information given by Matthew. But he has added a few things. Mark says Jesus chose these men so that He could send them out to preach. There is nothing to indicate that these men had any experience as preachers. Yet it is clear that Jesus could see this possibility in them.

Jesus knows if you are to be a preacher before you know it. So, I would suggest to anyone who thinks they should preach that it would be a good idea to ask Jesus what He thinks about that idea. And be sure to ask before you try to preach.

Mark also lets us know that Jesus gave Peter his name. His parents had named him Simon. Jesus gave a nickname to the sons of Zebedee. This causes me to wonder about a couple of things. Who was Zebedee? Does this matter? What was it about these men that caused Jesus to refer to them as the "sons of thunder?" Was this a compliment or a corrective measure taken by Jesus?

Once again, in the Gospel of Mark, Judas Iscariot is identified as the man who betrayed Jesus.

When Luke shared his list of these twelve men, he added an interesting point the others did not mention. This is his lead-in to the list of men we know as the disciples.

> *And when it was day, he called unto him his disciples: and of them he chose twelve, whom also he named apostles; Simon, (whom he also named Peter,) and Andrew his brother, James and John, Philip and Bartholomew, Matthew and Thomas, James the son of Alphaeus, and Simon called Zelotes, And Judas the brother of James, and Judas Iscariot, which also was the traitor. (Luke 6:13-16)*

Luke indicated there was a larger group of people who were known as His disciples. It was from this group of disciples that Jesus chose these twelve men who came to be known as apostles. If this was the only account of how these men came to hold such an important place in the ministry of Jesus, we would miss some intriguing information given to us in other places. That is to say, the choosing of these twelve men did not happen exactly as it appears in these verses in Luke.

I am only clarifying that this account in the Gospel of Luke is not intended as the complete story. I have stated numerous times that chronology is difficult to establish in the Gospels. I think this is a good example. We know from other Scriptures that Jesus had chosen a group of 70 other people and sent them out to minister.

Many of them were probably in this crowd. It is much too easy to focus on the multitudes that followed Jesus. We tend to forget that day by day, His inner circle was steadily growing. This is how the Holy Spirit works in every ministry, where He is allowed to take the lead.

I will not leave these statements just to trouble your mind. This passage from Luke may be speaking of the moment Jesus introduced these twelve men to a larger group of His followers. It may have been at this moment that Jesus made their role clearer to the larger group. I suspect much more happened that morning than is recorded in these verses.

We should not view these events as something spontaneous that happened in the middle of a church service. I don't think that Jesus suddenly stood up in the middle of one of His meetings and called out the names of twelve men and installed them as His apostles. Jesus was not that impulsive. His actions seem to have always been intentional. Numerous conversations had transpired between Jesus and these men before the event recorded in the book of Luke occurred. There is no question this happened, but many other things were involved that are not included in the text.

There are many places in Scripture where a single statement is made, and it is intended to be sufficient to express an important part of what took place. The writers of the Scripture passages often seem to leave out details that would be interesting but serve no real purpose. I believe the Holy Spirit instructed them to skip over these details.

One such example of this is the wedding where Jesus turned water into wine. Have you ever noticed this statement?

> *On the third day there was a wedding at Cana in Galilee, and the mother of Jesus was there. Jesus also was invited to the wedding* **with his disciples.** *When the wine ran out, the mother of Jesus said to him, "They have no wine." And Jesus said to her, "Woman, what does this have to do with me? My hour has not yet come." His mother said to the servants, "Do whatever he tells you." Now there were six stone water jars there for the Jewish rites of purification, each holding twenty or thirty gallons. Jesus said to the servants, "Fill the jars with water." And they filled them up to the brim.*
> *(John 2:1-7 – ESV)*

His Disciples

Jesus was *invited to the wedding with his disciples.* He already had disciples. This is considered to be the first miracle Jesus performed. It is also often referred to as the beginning of His ministry. Yet there were disciples. How many of "His Disciples" went with Him? Were any of them a part of this group of twelve men who became apostles? We will never know the answers to these questions.

Then why am I asking these questions? I am only asking because it seems Jesus would have wanted these twelve men to witness His first miracle. Were all twelve of them at the wedding? We don't know. But we can rest assured those twelve men saw the miracles the Holy Spirit knew it was important for them to see.

It is amazing how the Holy Spirit is always working.

Let's turn our attention now to the choosing of five of these disciples. The following passage from John's writings is lengthy. However, it is packed with the only real detail we have about these particular men. We are given the opportunity to see the transition that began to unfold from John the Baptist. At least to some degree, we can think of this as the record of how the ministry of the disciples began.

As I have indicated, these Scriptures do not mention all twelve disciples. We know extraordinarily little about how Jesus chose the other seven men not mentioned in these verses. In the next two chapters, I will share what is known about those men.

The next day again John was standing with two of his disciples, and he looked at Jesus as he walked by and said, "Behold, the Lamb of God!" The two disciples heard him say this, and they followed Jesus. Jesus turned and saw them following and said to them, "What are you seeking?" And they said to him, "Rabbi" (which means Teacher), "where are you staying?" He said to them, "Come and you will see." So they came and saw where he was staying, and they stayed with him that day, for it was about the tenth hour. One of the two who heard John speak and followed Jesus was Andrew, Simon Peter's brother. He first found his own brother Simon and said to him, "We have found the Messiah" (which means Christ). He brought him to Jesus. Jesus looked at him and said, "You are Simon the son of John. You shall be called Cephas" (which means Peter). The next day Jesus decided to go to Galilee. He found Philip and said to him, "Follow me." Now Philip was from Bethsaida, the city of Andrew and Peter. Philip found Nathanael and said to him, "We have found him of whom Moses in the Law and also the prophets wrote, Jesus of Nazareth, the son of Joseph." Nathanael said to him, "Can anything good come out of Nazareth?" Philip said to him, "Come and see." Jesus saw Nathanael coming toward him and said of him, "Behold, an Israelite indeed, in whom there is no deceit!" Nathanael said to him, "How do you know me?" Jesus answered him, "Before Philip called you, when you were under the fig tree, I saw you." Nathanael answered him, "Rabbi, you are the Son of God! You are the King of Israel!" Jesus answered him, "Because I said to you, 'I saw you under the fig tree,' do you believe? You will see greater things than these." And he said to him, "Truly, truly, I say to you, you will see heaven opened, and the angels of God ascending and descending on the Son of Man." (John 1:35-51 – ESV)

Four of the twelve disciples are mentioned by name. They are Andrew, Simon Peter, Philip, and Nathanael. My research indicates that Nathanael and Bartholomew are the same person. Perhaps that information will clarify things as we progress through this study.

Another individual is mentioned in this passage, but we are not given his name. Some sources assume this was John, but others do not. I believe it is correct to consider this the disciple known as John, and I will explain why.

The author of the Gospel of John mentions himself several times in his Gospel, but he never uses his name. John often calls himself the "disciple that Jesus loved" or simply the other disciple. In this passage, John does not refer to this fifth disciple as the "disciple that Jesus loved." However, in listing these disciples, John retains the same approach to concealing his identity found in other places in his book. So, I am basing my assumption on John's pattern of concealing his identity. It simply makes sense.

It is interesting to notice how this event happened as it is described by John. He mentions that these two men heard John the Baptist when he spoke about Jesus. Why would John make such a statement and not mention the man's name unless he was talking about himself?[22] This is an example of what I have just stated. If this is to be viewed as an act of humility, then I see no reason not to believe it is genuine.

John the Baptist was standing with two of his disciples when Jesus walked by, and when John the Baptist saw Jesus, he proclaimed: *"Behold, the Lamb of God!"* The two men with John the Baptist immediately began to follow Jesus. One of these was the John I have written about, and the other man's name was Andrew.

Shortly after the encounter between John the Baptist and Jesus, Andrew found his brother, Simon Peter, and told him they had found the Messiah. This appears to have happened quickly, but we cannot be certain. Peter joined the group, and now Andrew, the unnamed disciple (John), and Peter were following Jesus.

When these two men (Andrew and John) left John the Baptist and began following Jesus, this did not cause any jealousy in John the Baptist because this was his purpose in life. He was here to prepare the way of the Lord. This had been a challenging task. But the influence John the Baptist had been able to have on John and Andrew should be viewed as a significant aspect of preparing the way of the Lord. My conclusion is based on the position that John came to have in

His Disciples

the ministry of Jesus. And we must not forget that it was Andrew who brought his brother (Peter) to Jesus.

Peter gets a lot of criticism for always saying things when we think he should have been quiet. He seems to have been aggressive at times and maybe a little rambunctious. But, of all the disciples who later became apostles, it is Peter who leads the way beginning on the Day of Pentecost.

When we think of all that transpired in the life of Peter as he followed Jesus it may not at first occur to us to consider this as something that John the Baptist played a part in. However, as I have just pointed out it is entirely possible that had Andrew not been influenced by John the Baptist, we might not have ever heard of Peter.

I am not trying to stretch this out to some ridiculous limit. I am only wanting you to realize how important little things are in the Kingdom of God. I think eternity will surprise us in many ways.

All of the rewards will not go to the people who were public figures here on earth. There will be many moms and dads and friends that no one knew that God will reward for their faithfulness in building His Kingdom. You may be one of them.

If you carefully study the various places where the choosing of the disciples occurred, you will see different stories about how this all happened. I will come back to the account given by John momentarily and finish that story, but first, here is an example. This account leaves the impression that choosing the disciples was quite different from what the other writers have said. Is this a contradiction? I do not think so. I believe we have bits and pieces of a huge story, with each writer sharing the part that stood out to them. It would require far too many unfounded assumptions to try to put all of these pieces together into one story. Thus, I will leave it as it has been given to us.

> *One day as Jesus was standing by the Lake of Gennesaret, the people were crowding around him and listening to the word of God. He saw at the water's edge two boats, left there by the fishermen, who were washing their nets. He got into one of the boats, the one belonging to Simon, and asked him to put out a little from shore. Then he sat down and taught the people from the boat. When he had finished speaking, he said to Simon, "Put out into deep water, and let down the nets for a catch." Simon answered, "Master, we've worked hard all night and haven't caught anything. But because you say so, I will let down the nets." When they had done so, they caught such a large number of fish that their nets began to break. So they signaled their partners in the other boat to come and help them, and they came and filled both boats so full that they began to sink. When Simon Peter saw this, he fell at Jesus' knees and said, "Go away from me, Lord; I am a sinful man!" For he and all his companions*

were astonished at the catch of fish they had taken, and so were James and John, the sons of Zebedee, Simon's partners. Then Jesus said to Simon, "Don't be afraid; from now on you will fish for people." So they pulled their boats up on shore, left everything and followed him. (Luke 5:1-11 – NIV)

It seems obvious that Jesus and Peter knew each other because Jesus was using Simon Peter's boat. Other men were present, and their names are not mentioned. But, in this passage, we do have the names of Simon Peter and James and John, the sons of Zebedee.

I raised two questions earlier that I should now answer. Who was this man named Zebedee? He was a partner in the fishing business with Peter. Once again, this is a small thing that may seem inconsequential on the surface. Yet, look at how the Holy Spirit used it in the ministry of Jesus.

The sons of Zebedee became apostles, but Zebedee did not. We are not told why this man was not chosen. It may have been due to his other responsibilities. On the other hand, consider the possible conflict Jesus might have dealt with by having this father and his two sons working so closely with Him. We can learn a lot from that.

It seems apparent that the reason for the mention of Zebedee in the New Testament is because of his two sons and his wife. Zebedee was married to Salome. Mary, the mother of Jesus, and Salome were sisters. This made Zebedee[23] the uncle of Jesus and his sons were the cousins of Jesus. I trust you find these family connections as intriguing as I do. It always causes me to think about and reflect on who believed in Jesus and who was still unsure.

His mother and His aunt Salome, along With His uncle Zebedee and His cousins James and John, all believed in Him. These relationships were not just important, but they were significant in the ministry of Jesus and His disciples. They provide profound insight into the depth of His teachings and who He was. There is no question that Jesus loved His earthly family.

But why did Jesus call the sons of Zebedee the sons of thunder? This nickname is found in the following passage.

James the son of Zebedee and John the brother of James (to whom he gave the name Boanerges,[24] that is, Sons of Thunder); (Mark 3:17 – ESV)

It is commonly believed that Jesus gave these two men this nickname because of their reaction to the rejection Jesus had received from the people in the town of Samaria as they passed through.

When the days drew near for him to be taken up, he set his face to go to Jerusalem. And he sent messengers ahead of him, who went and entered a village of the Samaritans, to make preparations for him. But the people did not receive him, because his

face was set toward Jerusalem. And when his disciples James and John saw it, they said, "Lord, do you want us to tell fire to come down from heaven and consume them?"
(Luke 9:51-54 – ESV)

In those few verses, you can almost feel the tension between those who believed in Jesus and those who did not believe in Him. There was a longstanding hatred between the Jews and the Samaritans. It is spoken of and illustrated in the Gospels. By this time in His ministry, Jesus had said and done several things to show that this hatred was wrong. It needed to change. So, the last thing Jesus wanted was for these men who believed in Him to do what the Prophet Elijah had done when he called fire down from Heaven. It was not a matter of whether this could be done. It was a matter of whether it should be done.

Just because we can do something, this does not always mean we should. Not following this small expression of wisdom has caused many problems. Calling fire down from Heaven would have undone everything Jesus had accomplished. It could have also caused other problems, perhaps even the arrest and imprisonment of these men.

Jesus had this unique way of reminding His disciples of things in them that needed to change. It is as though He teased them as a way of reminding them of their shortcomings. He was molding them into the powerful men of God they became after they were filled with the Holy Ghost. Think of this nickname as an attitude adjustment. I am sure Jesus called these men by that nickname in front of the other disciples.

Matthew provides another glimpse into the fishing trip I spoke of earlier. He includes information not found in the book of Luke.

> *As He was walking by the Sea of Galilee, He noticed two brothers, Simon who is called Peter and Andrew his brother, throwing a dragnet into the sea, for they were fishermen. And He said to them, Come after Me [as disciples—letting Me be your Guide], follow Me, and I will make you fishers of men! At once they left their nets and became His disciples [sided with His party and followed Him]. And going on further from there He noticed two other brothers, James son of Zebedee and his brother John, in the boat with their father Zebedee, mending their nets and putting them right; and He called them. At once they left the boat and their father and joined Jesus as disciples [sided with His party and followed Him].*
> *(Matthew 4:18-22 – AMPC)*

The first four disciples clearly mentioned by name were Andrew, Peter, Philip, and Nathanael. In this passage, we have the names of two more disciples. We can now confirm that John and his brother James can be added to the list. The man named John, the brother of James and the son of Zebedee, is the same man named John who wrote the Gospel of John. He is the one who referred to himself in his writings in the Gospel of John as "the disciple whom Jesus loved." He never used his name in his writings. Thus, it can sometimes be difficult to figure out who John is talking about. Perhaps a list will be helpful.

> John can be identified in all of the following ways.
> He was the unnamed disciple of John the Baptist.
> He was the other man who was with Andrew.
> He was the disciple whom Jesus loved.
> He wrote the Gospel of John.
> He never used his name in his writing.
> He was the brother of James.
> He was the son of Zebedee.
> He was the cousin of Jesus.

The Jews had a habit of using the same name for numerous people, even when it was just a small group of people or if they were from the same town. Other names were certainly available. We do the same thing today, and it can get very confusing. They could be creative with names. We have several examples of this even in this list of twelve men. Yet several men were named John, just like several ladies were named Mary.

Before we return to the passage in the Gospel of John and look at how Philip and Nathanael became disciples, I must share these thoughts with you. Choosing the right people for places of leadership can never happen as it should without the guidance, wisdom, and help of the Holy Spirit.

As you read these stories it all appears so natural. They are just talking or fishing, and then they are telling their families they are going to follow Jesus. Jesus tells them they will become *fishers of men,* whatever that means, and off they go. I think the ultimate outcome, including the fact that over 2000 years later, we are still intrigued with these men and their story, lets us know there was much more going on than we might imagine.

Throughout the process of finding and choosing these twelve men, the transformative power of the Holy Ghost was at work, far beyond what meets the eye. They saw something in Jesus that drew them to Him. They did not understand who He was, but it was clear Jesus was a person they wanted to follow.

Jesus saw something in them that drew Him to them. He wanted them to follow Him and to come to know Him. This was the work of the Holy Ghost, a divine force that turned ordinary men into powerful disciples. They may not have had ministerial skills, but they were chosen and transformed by the Holy Ghost, just as we all must depend on the Holy Ghost.

It is also clear that none of these men had a history in the ministry as it was known in the Jewish tradition. Their fathers did not pave the way for them. In fact, this would not have been a possibility unless they had been in the priestly lineage. The selection of these men, who were not from a traditional ministerial background, is a testament to the ways of the Lord. Who Jesus was can be seen in so many of His decisions. He was the Son of man, and He believed in ordinary people. He still does!

Some of my friends in the ministry were fortunate enough to have fathers and mothers who were ministers. I am saying they were fortunate, because it allowed them to know many things it took some of the rest of us several years to learn. Whether or not having parents in the ministry is something we should think of as fortunate depends on the parents' character and reputation. The true value of what parents in the ministry provide has little to do with the size of their ministry. Of course, a lot does depend on what the next generation chooses to do in following the direction of the Holy Ghost.

No parent has ever had enough of the Holy Ghost to suffice for the next generation. The Kingdom of God does not function in that way. However, at times it does appear that some people think it does. It always makes me sad to see a young minister burdened with the task of trying to live up to (or overcome) what their parents have done. I am talking about the good and the bad, and I have seen both.

If these ordinary men Jesus chose could become powerhouses for God, then it is a testament to the potential for any man or woman called by God. If God could use them, He can use us. It may not be easy, but it is certainly possible, and this knowledge should empower and embolden us in our faith or ministry or whatever occupation or profession we may have. The Holy Ghost is available to all of us.

Who Do Men Say That I AM?

Now, let's look at how Philip and his brother Nathaniel got involved in the ministry of Jesus. This is one of the more interesting stories I have found about the selection of the twelve disciples. We can clearly see the Holy Spirit at work in the interaction between Jesus and Nathanael.

> *The next day Jesus decided to go to Galilee. He found Philip and said to him, "Follow me." Now Philip was from Bethsaida, the city of Andrew and Peter. Philip found Nathanael and said to him, "We have found him of whom Moses in the Law and also the prophets wrote, Jesus of Nazareth, the son of Joseph." Nathanael said to him, "Can anything good come out of Nazareth?" Philip said to him, "Come and see." Jesus saw Nathanael coming toward him and said of him, "Behold, an Israelite indeed, in whom there is no deceit!" Nathanael said to him, "How do you know me?" Jesus answered him, "Before Philip called you, when you were under the fig tree, I saw you." Nathanael answered him, "Rabbi, you are the Son of God! You are the King of Israel!" Jesus answered him, "Because I said to you, 'I saw you under the fig tree,' do you believe? You will see greater things than these." And he said to him, "Truly, truly, I say to you, you will see heaven opened, and the angels of God ascending and descending on the Son of Man." (John 1:43-51 – ESV)*

What is the rest of the story?

His Disciples

Did Jesus just wake up one morning and decide to go to Galilee? It certainly sounds that way. But I don't think so.

We often think we just decide to do things, and we are not aware that the Holy Spirit is directing our steps. We may figure this out later, but how much more productive could we be if we were aware of this direction from the Holy Ghost as it was happening? Jesus found Philip *and said to him, "Follow me."* About the only personal thing we know about this man is that he was from the same city as Andrew and Peter. Do you realize this would not have happened (at least not when it did and how it did) if Jesus had not decided to go to Galilee that day? This is called being led by the Holy Ghost.

> *The steps of a [good and righteous] man are directed and established by the LORD, And He delights in his way [and blesses his path].*
> *(Psalm 37:23 – AMP)*

In every encounter Jesus had during the selection of His twelve disciples, His steps were directed and established by His Father. The proof of this is the results. I do not just mean He was able to find twelve men. I mean, Jesus was able to find the right twelve men. We know because of what these men became.

Often, we want to see the end from the beginning. This almost never happens. As I have discussed this selection process and the kind of men Jesus chose, I hope you can see what an act of faith this was on the part of Jesus.

The manner in which you view that last statement says a lot about how you view the humanity of Jesus. Has it ever crossed your mind that Jesus needed faith? If you only see Jesus as the Son of God, then your answer will be no. Yet, when you begin to see Jesus as the Son of man, it broadens your perspective. It becomes easier to embrace the idea that Jesus was, in fact, our example in every respect.

He made the right choices. Yet, it took more than three years for Jesus to see the outcome of His choices.

When we look at the encounter Jesus had with Philip and see that this is reduced to the words *"Follow me,"* it would be possible to quickly pass over this as though it is nothing. That would be a huge mistake.

On many occasions, the Holy Spirit will touch the life of someone who then influences others, yet we know very little about that first person. We tend to like the superstars. We like the big names. I am not saying this is wrong. But I am saying that Heaven may get extremely exciting when we meet people we have never heard of and find out the powerful impact they had on the Kingdom of God. I think Philip is one of those people.

My conclusion is based on the way Philip dealt with Nathanael. Here is another part of this story that would be easy to pass over. At this point in the ministry of Jesus, there had been no resistance that we know about. Things were going along smoothly. This is the first person we know about who resisted the call to follow Jesus. *Nathanael said to him (Philip), "Can anything good come out of Nazareth?" Philip said to him, "Come and see."*

The response from Nathanael about Nazareth was that you did not want it to be known that you were from Nazareth. Nazareth was not a popular place. However, I would like to suggest that something else was going on. Think about the words Philip spoke to his brother. *Philip found Nathanael and said to him, "We have found him of whom Moses in the Law and also the prophets wrote, Jesus of Nazareth, the son of Joseph."*

These words are true. Philip was correct in what he said. However, when Nathanael met Jesus, we learn more about this man. When Jesus first saw Nathanael, He said: *"Behold, an Israelite indeed, in whom there is no deceit!" Nathanael said to him, "How do you know me?"*

It seems that if Nathanael was not a man who was willing to deceive others, he also was not a man who was going to allow himself to be deceived. Those two things go together. I do not deceive other people, and I hate to be deceived. I believe Nathanael was the same way.

Nathanael was just being careful. We can learn a lot from this man about checking things out before we get involved. I especially want you to notice that Nathanael's reaction did not upset Jesus. Jesus knew exactly what to do. He allowed the Holy Spirit to speak through Him the very words that would get the attention of Nathanael.

For Jesus to say, "I think I know you," or "You sure look familiar," or "Your brother has told me a lot about you," would not have been effective. What did work was something that the Holy Spirit knew that Philip would have never thought to mention to Jesus about his brother Nathanael.

All of us have certain opinions of ourselves. There are things we hope people see in us and believe about us. This is just human nature. However, this is powerful when some unknown person can express so clearly our personal view of ourselves upon first meeting us.

Nothing is more effective than a personal encounter with the Holy Ghost, especially if you have never heard anything about Him. I might add nothing is more powerful than a personal encounter with Jesus. And that is exactly what happened to Nathanael. They double-teamed this man.

It is intriguing that when Jesus saw Nathanael coming toward Him, **Jesus spoke the first word of knowledge[25] we know about in the ministry of Jesus.** That is noteworthy.

On numerous occasions after this, it was common for Jesus to have a word of knowledge or a word of wisdom for the person to whom He was speaking. We can learn a great deal as we examine these gifts from the Holy Ghost as they were manifested in His ministry. Often these words of wisdom and words of knowledge do not sound so important at first until you notice the context. This was a Holy Ghost inspired response to the negative attitude of Nathanael.

His Disciples

Jesus said: *"Behold, an Israelite indeed, in whom there is no deceit!"* That could be taken as a flowery compliment. Or it could be a true and accurate expression provided by the Holy Spirit regarding how this man felt about himself and how he wanted others to think of him. I have already been clear about which of these I consider it to be. But I hope you can see what an impact the right words had on Nathanael.

To Nathanael, this was more than flowery words. How could a man he had never met speak so directly and precisely what was in his heart? The evidence he felt that way is found in his response. *Nathanael said to him, "How do you know me?"*

By that simple statement, Jesus had made it clear He knew Nathanael. How could this be possible? We now know this was the work of the Holy Ghost in the ministry of Jesus.

I am quite sure Nathanael was not expecting what came next. These other four disciples were certainly getting a firsthand lesson in the gifts of the Holy Spirit.[26] As I have indicated, first, Jesus had a word of knowledge,[27] and then He made it known that He also was operating in the discerning of spirits.[28] This information is found in the words of Jesus. *"Before Philip called you, when you were under the fig tree, I saw you."*

It has often been said that the word discern[29] means to see. According to the *Collins Dictionary*, this is partially correct. This resource says it means to perceive by sight **or some other sense** or by the intellect: see, recognize, or apprehend. Notice that even this definition mentions "or some other sense" as part of the meaning they provide.

But the discerning[30] I am talking about happened in Jesus before He ever met Nathanael. It is defined much more accurately in the *Vines Expository Dictionary*. It is in this excellent resource that we find the information that tells us that "discerning of spirits is "a distinguishing, a clear discrimination, discerning, judging," it is translated as "discerning" in 1 Corinthians 12:10 of "discerning" spirits, judging by evidence whether they are evil or of God."

While that may be a lot to take in, it is particularly important. I will suggest that this man was not the only disciple that Jesus knew things about through this gift of the Spirit when He first chose them. Numerous examples of this same Holy Ghost-inspired wisdom are found in the ministry of Jesus. He often knew things about people that He did not learn from a natural, human source.

The gift of the discerning of spirits is essential for any ministry. Many ministries have been utterly ruined because the pastor, teacher, or evangelist fell prey to the deceitfulness of individuals they trusted. This could have been avoided if this gift of the Spirit had been functioning in their lives.

In the response Jesus made to Nathanael, we have a combination of gifts of the Spirit. Jesus knew Nathanael had been under a fig tree. That may seem small by itself. It could seem to be a lucky guess, but this information was cumulative, and Nathanael knew it was much more than a lucky guess. Jesus had already told him how he thought of himself. Jesus knew where he had been. The detail was very convincing. This could have scared this man away. But the spirit in which it was given made it acceptable.

Nathanael responded to Jesus with these words. *"Rabbi, you are the Son of God! You are the King of Israel!"* That was quite a declaration for someone who had just met Jesus. There was only one way Nathanael could have known this. It had to be a revelation[31] given to him by the Holy Spirit. I have often wondered if Nathanael knew this. Did Nathanael know the Holy Spirit had given him this insight? We are not told the answer.

Peter did not seem to know he had received a revelation when he declared that Jesus was the Son of God. Jesus had to teach him that this is what had happened. It might surprise you to know that people don't always know the Holy Spirit is working through them. But it happens very often.

I am not implying that this is a good thing. It is not. If we know the Holy Spirit is using us, we can be more available for Him to work through us.

**When the Holy Spirit is at work,
He will often speak to both parties.**

I mentioned a revelation that was given to Peter. At a later point in His ministry, Jesus had a conversation with His disciples about who He was. Jesus not only wanted to know what was being said about Him. He wanted to know who His disciples believed He was. This was not an ego trip. Jesus had been teaching His disciples. It was important for Him to know the degree to which the revelation of His true identity had become clear to them. It is this story that provided the motivation for this book. That should be obvious from the title of the book.

> *When Jesus came into the coasts of Caesarea Philippi, he asked his disciples, saying, Whom do men say that I the Son of man am? And they said, Some say that thou art John the Baptist: some, Elias; and others, Jeremias, or one of the prophets. He saith unto them, But whom say ye that I am? And Simon Peter answered and said, Thou art the Christ, the Son of the living God. (Matthew 16:13-16)*

After all the time Jesus had spent with these men and all the things He had taught them, there still appears to have been a hesitancy regarding His identity. In all fairness, Jesus did ask them who the people were saying He was. Yet, from His response to Peter, it seems clear Jesus also wanted to know if they fully understood who He was.

When Jesus put this question to His disciples about His identity, He had been teaching them for some time, and they had heard Him say many times who He was. He had explained this to them. When Nathanael was chosen as a disciple, he had heard none of this. For Nathanael to know this about

His Disciples

Jesus and say it when he first met Jesus is remarkable. This provides a wonderful example of the work of the Holy Spirit in the ministry of Jesus and in the life of Nathanael.

We don't know much about Nathanael. However, as I have been sharing with you, it is possible to see that he was a truly remarkable man. He is hardly mentioned in Scripture. Some of the early church fathers say glowing things about him, which we cannot prove, but what follows in the words of Jesus is a remarkable word of wisdom[32] given to this man. Some would call this a prophecy,[33] but that is a discussion for later.

> *Jesus answered him, "Because I said to you, 'I saw you under the fig tree,' do you believe? You will see greater things than these." And he said to him, "Truly, truly, I say to you, you will see heaven opened, and the angels of God ascending and descending on the Son of Man."*
> *(John 1:50-51 – ESV)*

We are now confronted with a question. Did this word of wisdom ever happen? I believe it did. I can't point you to a story in the Bible that says this in a specific way. However, this we can be sure of, Nathanael would have been present when Jesus ascended into Heaven.

> *And when he had said these things, as they were looking on, he was lifted up, and a cloud took him out of their sight. And while they were gazing into heaven as he went, behold, two men stood by them in white robes,*

> *and said, "Men of Galilee, why do you stand looking into heaven? This Jesus, who was taken up from you into heaven, will come in the same way as you saw him go into heaven." (Acts 1:9-11 – ESV)*

Heaven was opened that day. What a marvelous site that must have been. Two angels came and spoke to the men who were there. We are not given the names of every person who was present that day when Jesus ascended back into Heaven. We are told that Peter was there and the eleven were there. **Nathanael was there.**[34] Most definitely, Nathanael was in the upper room when the Holy Ghost was poured out. He was there when Peter began to preach. And Nathanael definitely saw Jesus as He ascended into Heaven.

It is hard to accept that only two angels showed up for the ascension. If a multitude of the Heavenly Host[35] accompanied the birth of Jesus, it is reasonable to think a multitude came to escort Him back into His place in Heaven. Remember, Jesus said He could have called legions of angels to protect Him when they arrested Him.

I am not saying the Biblical record is incorrect. I simply think it is possible that the people there only saw two of the many angels who came to escort Jesus home to His Father. Jesus was returning to Heaven victorious over the devil. He had set in motion the greatest thing to happen on this earth since its creation. Those in attendance may not have recognized the significance of this moment. However, I am sure the angels did. The Son of God was coming home.

Perhaps you noticed that these two beings were called men. In the Bible it is not unusual to find angels referred to as men. This happens often enough that we are even told we may see them and not be aware we are seeing angels. Thus, I believe Nathanael saw what Jesus had told him he would see.

Chapter 12
His Other Six Choices

Just because the other six disciples are hardly mentioned in the Bible, this does not make them less important. I can't explain why we don't know more about them, but I am sure there is a good reason.

Their names are Matthew, Thomas, James The Less, Simon The Zealot, Judas, Not Iscariot (this man had three names), and Judas - The Traitor. What do we know about these six men?

Let's begin with Matthew. Tax collectors were some of the most despised people in all of Israel. They often lied and cheated the people of Israel out of money to make themselves rich and to gain favor with the Roman government. Yet Jesus chose a tax collector to be one of His disciples. Jesus knew there was hope for anyone who would believe in Him. We can understand a little more about Matthew by reading the story of another tax collector named Zacchaeus.

> *Then Jesus entered and passed through Jericho. Now behold, there was a man named Zacchaeus who was a chief tax collector, and he was rich. And he sought to see who Jesus was, but could not because of the crowd, for he was of short stature. So he ran ahead and climbed up into a sycamore tree to see Him, for He was going to pass that way. And when Jesus came to the place, He looked up and saw him, and said to him, "Zacchaeus, make haste and come down, for today I must stay at your house." So he made haste and came down, and received Him joyfully. But when they saw it, they all complained, saying, "He has gone to be a guest with a man who is a sinner." Then Zacchaeus stood and said to the Lord, "Look, Lord, I give half of my goods to the poor; and if I have taken anything from anyone by false accusation, I restore fourfold." And Jesus said to him, "Today salvation has come to this house, because he also is a son of Abraham; for the Son of Man has come to seek and to save that which was lost." (Luke 19:1-10 – NKJV)*

We are not provided with this kind of detail about Matthew. We do know that he, too, was a tax collector. We also know that Matthew did not go looking for Jesus. Instead, Jesus found him. When Jesus asked Matthew to follow Him it appears that Matthew did so and did it without question. How much did Matthew understand? We do not know for certain. I will say that many people begin their relationship with Jesus with little understanding. So, what does Matthew tell us about his encounter with Jesus?

I have inserted a little more information about Matthew to help answer this question.

> *As Jesus passed on from there, he saw a man called Matthew sitting at the tax booth, and he said to him, "Follow me." And he rose and followed him. And as Jesus reclined at table in the house, behold, many tax collectors and sinners came and were reclining with Jesus and his disciples.*
> *(Matthew 9:9-10 – ESV)*

It should be obvious there is a huge gap between the information found in those first two sentences and the next sentence that speaks of Matthew reclining at a table.

To keep this from being confusing I will state clearly that **Jesus did go to the house that belonged to Zacchaeus.** Jesus said He would do this. According to Luke's account Jesus actually stayed in the home of Zacchaeus as a guest. When Jesus saw Zacchaeus in the tree that day, He invited Himself to the home of Zacchaeus, and He was welcomed there. This was not merely metaphorical.

Jesus also went to the home of Matthew. If we can make anything similar to a chronological sequence from the order in which these stories appear in the book of Luke, Matthew met Jesus before Zacchaeus did.

While we are not told this in the Biblical text, I am willing to assert that these stories are about men who were loaded down with guilt. They were hated and ostracized. To find total acceptance from another Jew was remarkable to them.

The curiosity this must have stirred among this house of thieves must have been prodigious. How remarkable that someone could really care about them? How unusual that Jesus could feel comfortable among them and yet be so clear about what was right and what was wrong. In their minds and hearts, this was a huge deal. It had never happened. This was the work of the Holy Spirit.

Jesus went to Matthew's house and was so comfortable there that He reclined at a *table in the house* with some of the other tax collectors. And regardless of how it all happened, Jesus was much too friendly with the tax collectors to suit the religious crowd. Matthew's Gospel also states that His disciples were with Him.

How did all of this come to be? After Jesus encountered Matthew and called him to be one of His disciples, there was a meeting of some sort at the home of Matthew. Jesus attended this meeting. The Bible says many tax collectors and sinners were at the meeting in Matthew's house. The disciples that Jesus had already chosen were also in attendance. Something very consequential was taking place. This close association with tax collectors was unheard of among the Jews.

We don't know what they talked about in this meeting, but I can't help but believe Jesus did most of the talking. Could it be that Matthew invited Jesus to his house just so his tax collector friends could meet Him? I think this is likely. What about Zacchaeus? Was he there? From the way the story is written in the book of Luke, I must conclude that Zacchaeus was not present. This man *sought to see who Jesus was, but could not because of the crowd, for he was of short stature. So he ran ahead and climbed up into a sycamore tree to see Him, for He was going to pass that way.*

What makes me curious is how Zacchaeus knew enough about Jesus that he became so intent on seeing him that he was willing to climb up in a tree to make it happen. Could it be that some of the tax collectors who served under Zacchaeus were in that meeting in the home of Matthew? Zacchaeus is called a *chief tax collector.* He was a contractor who hired people to collect taxes.

It is likely that a number of these people who worked for Zacchaeus would have known Matthew and would have been at his house when Jesus was there. Perhaps they had been talking about Jesus, and Zacchaeus heard them and became curious.

Considering that the information I have quoted thus far about Matthew's first meeting with Jesus was provided by the same Matthew who became an apostle, provides an open window into this man's heart. Matthew, the former tax collector, wrote what we have as the first of the four Gospels. Yet, he only mentions himself when he provides a list of the twelve apostles. How uncommon and how sad that we don't see more of this attitude today.

Humility had become an earmark of this man's life. That is an amazing thing to say about a man who had once been so brazen in his arrogance and sin. What a dramatic change! I am calling him brazen based on what we know about typical tax collectors. He was more like Zacchaeus than we might think. Both of these men had been forgiven of much, and, as such, they were very grateful. Luke provides more detail about this meal Jesus had with the other tax collectors.

> *After these things He went out and saw a tax collector named Levi (Matthew), sitting at the tax office. And He said to him, "Follow Me." So he left all, rose up, and followed Him. Then Levi gave Him a great feast in his own house. And there were a great number of tax collectors and others who sat down with them. And their scribes and the Pharisees complained against His disciples, saying, "Why do You eat and drink with tax collectors and sinners?" Jesus answered and said to them, "Those who are well have no need of a physician, but those who are sick. I have not come to call the righteous, but sinners, to repentance."*
> (Luke 5:27-35 – NKJV)

Jesus knew that the way into the heart of many tax collectors was through the gratitude of one tax collector who had been set free. The forgiveness of sin and the release from guilt and condemnation is powerful. As you can see from our study thus far, one brother who had found Jesus led another brother to Him. Then, one fisherman who had found Jesus

His Other Six Choices

led another fisherman to Him. And so, it is with tax collectors as well. How many people did Zacchaeus bring to Jesus?

Today, we often see this same chain of events. What liberal person, what perverted individual, what drug addict, what actor, what billionaire, or any other individual will be the one whom the Holy Ghost will reach and use to ignite the next Great Awakening? It has happened every time there has been a great revival, and it will happen again. It happened with the Full Gospel Businessmen's Fellowship. It happened with the Jesus movement. The Holy Ghost knows how to make it happen again.

The next man chosen by Jesus was Thomas. He is mentioned in each of the Gospels, where the twelve apostles are listed by name. Yet it is only in the book of John that we find out anything about him. Thomas is known as a doubter and an extremely negative person who worried a lot. Jesus came to save us all, and it appears that the Holy Ghost directed Jesus to choose His apostles in a similar fashion. This is what we know about Thomas.

Then Thomas, who is called the Twin, said to his fellow disciples, "Let us also go, that we may die with Him." (John 11:16 – NKJV)

I have chosen not to use sources other than the Bible, accordingly, we do not know anything about that twin. Some early church fathers wrote stories about Thomas, which may or may not be reliable. I have not included those in this book.

Who Do Men Say That I AM?

As I pointed out in a previous chapter, a dear close friend of Jesus had died. Jesus needed to travel through a dangerous area to go to His friend. When Jesus mentioned taking a trip to where His friend had lived, Thomas, knowing how dangerous things could get, did not specifically mention protecting Jesus. He said he would go with Jesus, and he encouraged the others to go. Then, Thomas proceeded to talk about dying with Jesus. I wonder if Jesus rebuked him for those remarks. You may know someone who is that negative in their thinking. God loves them, too. This is not the end of the story of Thomas. He was still around after the Resurrection of Jesus, but it was not because he believed.

> *Now Thomas, called the Twin, one of the twelve, was not with them when Jesus came. The other disciples therefore said to him, "We have seen the Lord." So he said to them, "Unless I see in His hands the print of the nails, and put my finger into the print of the nails, and put my hand into His side, I will not believe." And after eight days His disciples were again inside, and Thomas with them. Jesus came, the doors being shut, and stood in the midst, and said, "Peace to you!" Then He said to Thomas, "Reach your finger here, and look at My hands; and reach your hand here, and put it into My side. Do not be unbelieving, but believing." And Thomas answered and said to Him, "My Lord and my God!" Jesus said to him, "Thomas, because you have seen Me, you have believed. Blessed are those who have not seen and yet have believed."*
> (John 20:24-29 – NKJV)

It is easy for us to be critical of the doubt that Thomas experienced. We have never met this man. We don't know what may have transpired in His life before he met Jesus that made him so negative and doubtful. One good thing we do know about Thomas is that something kept drawing Thomas back to Jesus, even when he was not sure it was Jesus.

It must have shocked Thomas when Jesus appeared in the room and the doors were shut. I think it would shock anybody. It must have shocked Thomas when Jesus quoted Him. Once again, we find the gift of the Spirit that Paul called the word of knowledge functioning in Jesus. Only this time, it is the risen Lord. What mattered most was that now Thomas believed.

We can appreciate those words spoken to Thomas that day. Jesus revealed some information we might not have otherwise known. Others may have recorded it in their writings, but it is especially meaningful to know that Jesus said those nail prints and those scars were still in His body. Even now, those scars are visible.

Jesus does not bear those scars to prove who He is. He carries those scars to remind those of us who believe in Him of the wonderful things He did for us. Though we have never seen Him, they speak very loudly of His love. Those scars express how much God cares for the lost and the suffering.

Thomas believed because he saw Jesus. He saw what the crucifixion had done to Jesus. We have not seen these things.

Yet we believe! We believe because the Word of God says these things are true. And to that belief, Jesus has attached a great blessing. Jesus included us that day when He uttered these beautiful words of promise.

> *Jesus said: Blessed are those who have not seen and yet have believed. (John 20:20 – NKJV)*

Little is known about the next three men Jesus chose as His disciples. However, I will share what I have found in the Word of God.

These three men are James, the son of Alphaeus, Simon the Zealot, and Judas, the son of James.

The only thing the Bible tells us about James, the son of Alphaeus, is his name. It is found in this passage.

> *Matthew and Thomas; James the son of Alphaeus, and Simon called the Zealot; Judas the son of James, and Judas Iscariot who also became a traitor.*
> *(Luke 6:15-16 – NKJV)*

The same reference to James, the son of Alphaeus, is found in Matthew 10:3, Mark 3:18, and Acts 1:13. In Mark 15:40, it is stated that the mother of James was named Mary. This same verse, along with Mark 15:47, mentions Joses, his brother. Joses was not an apostle, but he is mentioned often and must have been a devoted follower of Jesus. We also know that James, the son of Alphaeus, was given a nickname, which we find in Mark 15:40. He is referred to as James the Less! Don't you wonder what the word "Less" is all about?

> *There were also women looking on from afar, among whom were Mary Magdalene, Mary the mother of James the Less and of Joses, and Salome. (Mark 15:40 – NKJV)*

I don't know why this man was given this nickname. The most sensible explanation I have found is that the man was rather small in stature. Since we have no picture, that may or may not be true. To be included as one of the original twelve apostles is a great honor, no matter what they called him.

There are no negative reports about James the Less. He was in the upper room and was filled with the Holy Ghost. And he definitely saw the risen Jesus. It will be interesting to talk with him when we meet him in Heaven. Many in the Kingdom of God have a similar nature as this humble man.

The next name on the list is a man named Simon the Zealot, or, as some record, "Simon called the Zealot." This is the same man who is called "Simon the Canaanite" in Matthew 10:4 and in Mark 3:18.

When Simon is called "Simon the Canaanite," this could lead us to believe that this is a reference to the place of his birth or at least his hometown. This was a common way of expressing a person's name. We do not have any information to support the idea that Simon was from that region. *Strong* provides us with the fact that the word "Canaanite" is equal to calling him a zealous man.[36]

All we know about this disciple is that he had once been a member of an extremist group with a fierce hatred for Rome. These people were known to be extremely aggressive and could be militant and even violent. This may have been his past, but I do not see anything in the Bible to indicate that he remained that way as a disciple.

Judas, the son of James is the man who had three names. In the Gospel of Matthew chapter 10 and verse three, this man is called "Lebbaeus."[37] In this same verse, we also learn that his surname was "Thaddaeus."[38] You will find this information if you read the notes in *Strong's Concordance*. Judas, Lebbaeus, and Thaddaeus are all the same person.

Some scholars go so far as to believe that this was the brother of Jesus and that He is also the author of the book of the Bible, which bears the name Jude. I think it is a bit of a stretch to claim this man was the brother of Jesus. After all, the Bible does name his father, and it is not Joseph. His father's name was James.

When Peter spoke to the Gentiles in the house of Cornelius, he made some statements that I believe applied to the choosing of the twelve disciples. While this statement has been applied in other ways, I certainly think it fits the disciples. Give this some thought, and I think you will agree.

> *Then Peter opened his mouth, and said, Of a truth I perceive that God is no respecter of persons… How God anointed Jesus of Nazareth with the Holy Ghost and with power: who went about doing good, and healing all that were oppressed of the devil; for God was with him. (Acts 10:34-38 – KJV)*

Peter had received a revelation from the Holy Ghost that *God is no respecter of persons: But in every nation he that feareth him, and worketh righteousness, is accepted with him.* Jesus demonstrated this in His choice of the disciples.

Therefore, when Peter said God anointed Jesus of Nazareth with the Holy Ghost and with power, *who went about doing good,* choosing men like Matthew and Thomas and all of the other disciples was a great part of the *"doing good"* Peter was speaking about that day.

Thus, we have twelve men, each who, in his own right, was unique. It is interesting to observe that these men represent twelve vastly different personalities. At the very least, we can conclude that Jesus desired these men to be living proof that God loves every person and that He is capable and powerful enough to change anyone who is open and receptive to His love.

Even more intriguing than the changes that occurred in each of these men is how the love of God was shed abroad in their hearts. It caused them to get along, and this love created an inseparable bond among the eleven that remained after the crucifixion.

> *And when they had entered, they went up to the upper room, where they were staying, Peter and John and James and Andrew, Philip and Thomas, Bartholomew and Matthew, James the son of Alphaeus and Simon the Zealot and Judas the son of James. (Acts 1:13 – ESV)*

These eleven men stayed with Jesus throughout His entire earthly ministry. However, when Jesus was hanging on the cross, only one of the disciples was there.

> *When Jesus saw his mother and the disciple whom he loved standing nearby, he said to his mother, "Woman, behold, your son!" Then he said to the disciple, "Behold, your mother!" And from that hour the disciple took her to his own home. (John 19:26-27 – ESV)*

The *disciple whom he loved* was John. A strong bond had developed between John and Jesus. It is commonly believed among Biblical scholars that John was the youngest of the twelve apostles. How much younger we do not know. What is clear from reading the Gospels is that John seems to have always been there. Every Bible student has heard the names of Peter, James, and John mentioned many times. It is this John that is the disciple Jesus loved.

These words spoken by Jesus when He was hanging on the cross take on a more significant meaning when we realize **the disciple spoken of was not Mary's son.** If history is correct, John was her nephew. Mary was his aunt, not his mother. It is interesting that Jesus did not ask for one of His brothers to take care of their mother.

Instead, Jesus instructed His cousin, John, to care for His mother. Jesus still could not count on His family. It took the resurrection to change their hearts. But don't be too critical of the natural family of Jesus. It took His resurrection to change our hearts as well.

Of all the things taking place in those closing moments before the death of Jesus something incredibly special between these two individuals occurred. John embraced Mary as his mother, and from that hour, *the disciple took her to his own home.* John treated Mary like she was his own mother. It appears that Mary lived with John until her death.

Chapter 13
His Betrayer

There is only one remaining disciple to talk about. In all of the references to this man in the lists of disciples, he is known as the traitor. His name was Judas Iscariot. I suppose every Bible student has had the same questions about this man. Why did Jesus choose him? Didn't Jesus know what kind of man he was? When did Jesus discover it was Judas who would betray him? I am sure these are answers we would all like to have.

One of the most interesting things about this man is how successful he was at not arousing any suspicion about himself among the other disciples. So, if a deceptive friend has harmed you, you are not alone.

I think this way about Judas Iscariot because the other disciples did not immediately know who would betray Jesus when the subject came up. Surely, they were familiar with the prophecies about Jesus. Yet they had not yet grasped the reality and the gravity of this action of betrayal.

I am basing my conclusions on the very words of these other disciples.

> *When it was evening, he reclined at the table with the twelve. And as they were eating, he said, "Truly, I say to you, one of you will betray me." And they were very sorrowful and began to say to him one after another, "Is it I, Lord?" He answered, "He who has dipped his hand in the dish with me will betray me. The Son of Man goes as it is written of him, but woe to that man by whom the Son of Man is betrayed! It would have been better for that man if he had not been born."*
> *(Matthew 26:20-24 – ESV)*

This statement leaves the impression that most of them (if not all of them) were asking if they were the person Jesus meant. The other disciples did not know who Jesus was talking about. Had they known, they would never have asked if they were the ones to betray Him.

Jesus knew it was Judas Iscariot. He had known this all along. I realize those may be shocking words, but they are true. I will show you the proof.

One day when Jesus preached one of His powerful messages in the Synagogue, He was talking about what we have come to call communion. The message was about what His broken body and the shedding of His blood would do for them if they accepted it. In the record of that event, we are told Jesus knew it would be Judas who would betray Him.

Let's take this step by step and I will show you the evidence. Judas is not named in this story. But it is clear who He was talking about.

> *So Jesus said to them, "Truly, truly, I say to you, unless you eat the flesh of the Son of Man and drink his blood, you have no life in you. (John 6:53 – ESV)*

Those who heard Jesus speak took His words literally. At that moment they had no revelation of what Jesus was talking about. This included some of His disciples. And this was their reaction.

> *When many of his disciples heard it, they said, "This is a hard saying; who can listen to it?" But Jesus, knowing in himself that his disciples were grumbling about this, said to them, "Do you take offense at this? Then what if you were to see the Son of Man ascending to where he was before? It is the Spirit who gives life; the flesh is no help at all. The words that I have spoken to you are spirit and life. But there are some of you who do not believe." (For Jesus knew from the beginning who those were who did not believe, and who it was who would betray him.) (John 6:60-64 – ESV)*

This is astonishing. *(For Jesus knew from the beginning who those were who did not believe, and who it was who would betray him.)*

The writer mentions *those who did not believe* and *who it was who would betray him.* We now know after the fact that the first part is at least a reference to Thomas, as well as some others. Thomas said that he did not believe and would not believe that Jesus had risen from the dead until he saw the evidence. Jesus knew this about Thomas from the beginning. It takes a while for many people to believe.

This raises some interesting questions about Judas. Did Judas ever believe any of the things Jesus taught? Was he ever following Jesus for the right reasons?

Jesus chose Judas Iscariot knowing all along this man had a deceitful heart. We are not provided any details regarding what happened when Jesus chose Judas Iscariot as a disciple. It is hard to say much about him without the use of speculation. Knowing the nature of the Lord Jesus, it is not too far-fetched to think that Jesus was willing to do anything to give this man a chance to change. There are prophecies about Judas that are incredibly detailed. Jesus knew them all. I believe the Holy Ghost revealed to Jesus exactly who this person was.

Some have claimed that God predestined Judas Iscariot to be a traitor. I find that extremely hard to believe. It simply does not fit with my view of God. I always return to this verse when my thoughts are turned to such matters.

The Lord is not slack concerning his promise, as some men count slackness; but is longsuffering to us-

> *ward, not willing that any should perish, but that all should come to repentance. (2 Peter 3:9)*

My theology does not fit very well with either the Calvinists or those who hold to the doctrine of Arminianism. I find truth and error in both camps.

Many of those who are Calvinists claim that Judas Iscariot was born to betray Jesus. Some of them do not believe that Jesus died for people like Judas. Too many Scriptures state otherwise for me to accept that notion. Certainly, not the least of these is found in these verses.

> *For God so loved the world, that he gave his only begotten Son, that whosoever believeth in him should not perish, but have everlasting life. For God sent not his Son into the world to condemn the world; but that the world through him might be saved. (John 3:16-17)*

Did Judas Iscariot not fit the definition of *whosoever*, or does that word have a meaning I do not understand?

Those who hold tenaciously to the views of Arminianism would say that Judas Iscariot chose to betray Jesus. They believe this was entirely his choice. I find that as difficult to accept as the idea that Judas was born to betray Jesus. He may have plotted to do this for some time. However, the following statements show that Judas had significant evil help in this betrayal.

> *As soon as Judas took the bread, Satan entered into him. So Jesus told him, "What you are about to do, do quickly." (John 13:27 – NIV)*

The thoughts of a well-known and highly respected Calvinist will provide some insight into how some think about Judas Iscariot. His name is Charles Spurgeon.

Included in the autobiography of Charles Spurgeon is a copy of a sermon he preached titled "A Defense of Calvinism." This was one of his many attempts to defend what he believed. The sermon is found in Volume 1 of his autobiography. This sermon does not mention Judas by name, but it does provide some insight into the way a Calvinist thinks. This quote appears on page nine of this volume. The entire autobiography is readily available on the internet.

> That God predestines and yet that man is responsible, are two facts that few can see clearly. They are believed to be inconsistent and contradictory to each other. If then, I find taught in one part of the Bible that everything is foreordained, that is true, and if I find, in another Scripture, that man is responsible for all his actions, that is true, and it is only my folly that leads me to imagine that these two truths can ever contradict each other. I do not believe they can ever be welded into one upon any earthly anvil, but they certainly shall be one in eternity. They are two lines that are so nearly

parallel that the human mind which pursues them farthest will never discover that they converge, but they do converge, and they will meet somewhere in eternity, close to the throne of God, whence all truth doth spring.

I do not believe that one part of the Bible can contradict another part. The only satisfactory way I have found to resolve this conflict is to admit that there are many things I still do not understand. Charles Spurgeon and I agree on that point. He calls it "folly" to think there is a contradiction. I suppose it is folly to fret over those things we don't understand.

There are passages of scripture that support the idea of "some" things being foreordained in the lives of "some" people. **However, none of these declare that this applies to everything and every person in all circumstances.** There are also verses that make it clear we will be held responsible for our actions. **None of these verses say we are responsible for all of the things that happen in our lives. Neither extreme is found in the Bible.**

I have the utmost respect for this great man of God. Certainly, I do not want to misstate what he has written, nor do I want to misrepresent his intended meaning. I fully acknowledge that he is saying this is a conflict he had come to accept in that we can't resolve it in this life. Ultimately, he decided, much like I have, not to see these things as conflicting. I have also made that decision about other passages of Scripture.

What amazes me is his manner of interpreting the Word of God in this sermon. I will repeat the portion I want to address and provide the context. I will also highlight the troublesome words.

"**If** then, I find taught in one part of the Bible that **everything** is foreordained, that is true, and **if** I find, in another Scripture, that man is responsible for **all** his actions, that is true, and it is only my folly that leads me to imagine that these two truths can ever contradict each other." These statements baffle me because Spurgeon himself seems to question his own argument. He began each statement with the word **if**. He must have known he could not find such statements in the Bible.

There are Scriptures that do appear, as Spurgeon has suggested, but their scope is limited. **It is never all and everything!** These statements can be resolved by carefully comparing the Scriptures. Charles Spurgeon was a man of great intellect. To say He carefully studied the Bible does not do justice to the way this man lived. This was his life. Many consider him to be a great scholar and a marvelous preacher. Thus, I wonder about his relationship with the Holy Spirit. I will not judge him. I do not have that right. I only wonder why he could not see what seems to be so obvious to me.

It must be that Spurgeon lived and died with this internal conflict. He favored the Calvinist view. It is his honesty that causes me to respect him. I brought Spurgeon into this discussion of Judas Iscariot for a specific reason.

Speaking of these two different views, he said: "I do not believe they can ever be welded into one upon any earthly anvil, but they certainly shall be one in eternity." Many doctrinal differences are exactly as he has stated. He described them as "two lines that are so nearly parallel we will not resolve them in this life. But they will be resolved in eternity."

One example of this conflict (which Spurgeon makes no mention of in this sermon) can be found in a discussion of the tragic life of Judas Iscariot. The true believer in the Arminian doctrine would say Judas could have made another choice. They would say being a traitor was his choice. He was not coerced. I find that hard to accept. He seemed destined to do what he did. The prophecies had been given.

A true Calvinist would say that Judas was born to betray Jesus. He had no choice. This was his foreordained role on this earth. They might go so far as to say Judas was necessary for there to be a crucifixion, so this was the will of God. Would Spurgeon say these things? I don't know. From the content of the quote I provided, it does not seem that he would, but I may be mistaken because I have not read all of his sermons.

The devil did not "make" Judas do what he did. But he certainly helped him do it. And as he always does, once the evil deed had been done, then the devil left Judas to take all the blame and ultimately take his own life.

Early in the morning, all the chief priests and the elders of the people made their plans how to have

> *Jesus executed. So they bound him, led him away and handed him over to Pilate the governor. When Judas, who had betrayed him, saw that Jesus was condemned, he was seized with remorse and returned the thirty pieces of silver to the chief priests and the elders. "I have sinned," he said, "for I have betrayed innocent blood." "What is that to us?" they replied. "That's your responsibility."*
> (Matthew 27:1-4 – NIV)

We must not take lightly the remorse that Judas felt.

The Greek word, which has been translated in the NIV as remorse[39], means to have regret after the fact. Judas would have changed this if he could have. That was not possible. He took the money back in what appears to have been an act of remorse, but it did not matter. Some things in life are that way. That does not mean it was predestined. I think it is folly to assume that God had preordained this in the life of this man. So, what are we to do with this issue?

God knows everything. God knows what will happen long before it occurs. This was true of the fall of man. This was true of Israel turning her back on God. It is true of the people we have known who did things we can't understand. God always knows what will happen. I wonder what pain this must bring to the heart of a loving Heavenly Father.

God has had a direct influence on my life from the time of my birth until now. Could I have lived a different life?

I don't know, and I really don't want to know. What I do know is that I have made many decisions over the years, and I have lived with the results or consequences, as the case may be. Has there always been an unseen hand guiding me, and I did not know it? If so, there certainly have been plenty of times when it would have been great to know this. What I do know is that the Holy Spirit has always been with me, speaking to me often but always allowing me to make my own choices.

For those who have been deep in sin and God touched them, redeemed them, and made them His very own, I am so glad. Was this totally God's decision? I do not think so.

I find the words written by Charles Spurgeon that I have quoted here to be an attempt at a very eloquent way of saying there are just some things we will never figure out. I may be wrong, but out of respect for his legacy, I will accept them in that way. There must be some things we are not meant to know. Moses had these words of wisdom for us, and we should always remember them.

> *The secret things belong unto the* Lord *our God: but those things which are revealed belong unto us and to our children forever, that we may do all the words of this law. (Deuteronomy 29:29)*

Chapter 14
My Conclusions

As you probably noticed, the word used most often in this book is the word "relationship." This was not by accident. In so many ways, one of two things will happen in all of our lives. Either our relationships define us, or we define our relationships. This is much more than a matter of control. It is much more than a matter of personality. I think it is by design because those relationships can help us become the person God wants us to be, or they can do a lot to prevent it.

I am inclined to think this way because at the heart of it all is the matter of who we really are. Too many people never figure this out. They seem content to have relationships with people who like them, regardless of the character of the supposed friend.

We live in a very confused world. It is an extremely complicated world. In so many ways, I feel sorry for those who are just now graduating from High School or college. When I was their age, I knew what I wanted to do with my life. I had plans, and I began to pursue them aggressively. That does not mean that I was ready to do any of them. And it does not mean I had everything figured out. It does mean I had to move away from relationships I had enjoyed for years and then form new relationships.

I know this happens to many people, but the outcome is not the same. Where at one point in life, a person may have been surrounded by the right kind of people, it changed with the major decisions they made. And with these changes came many other bad choices. Yet others move from one set of great relationships to even stronger and more spiritually mature relationships. I did the latter. It certainly was not because I knew all of this or had everything out.

But I did know myself well enough to know that what I wanted to do was within my reach. It was possible if I only did certain things. I knew I needed to be around the right kind of people. They had to be positive people. I wanted a better life, and I wanted to be with people who believed this was possible. Something in me told me this was right.

I needed to get as prepared as possible to do whatever God wanted me to do. Then, I knew I was going to need to work hard. But most of all, I knew I needed the direction of the Holy Ghost. I needed His favor, and I needed to be sure I heard His voice and then followed what He told me to do. And the first of these directions had a lot to do with the relationships I formed.

My Conclusions

It was not as though some person or some group of people had told me these steps to take. It was the relationships I had as a child that had somehow formed these thoughts inside of me. I now know this was the work of the Holy Spirit. But I did not understand that until many years later. I had a godly mother, and I always went to church. This does not mean my mother was perfect or that my church was perfect. I had a Pastor that I admired. And once again, it was not because he was perfect.

My mother did a lot to ensure I had the right relationships. I only associated with kids and adults who believed like I believed. And somehow all of those relationships ultimately helped to define who I became.

I don't want to make this sound as though my life was perfectly planned out for me. It wasn't. I grew into the person God wanted me to be. And I am sure those relationships I had as a child and later as a teenager had a great deal to do with who I am today. Sadly, it may be that the greatest proof of what I am saying is found in the lives of those who did not have the advantage of the relationships I had. It saddens me to know that many from my past went a completely different direction in their adult lives. Things could have been much better for them.

As I look back on my life, it all seems simple now. But it sure was not simple then. There were many days through the years when I honestly did not know how things were going to work out. It did not always turn out the way I thought it should or the way I wanted it to. But life has been good, and more than that, God has been good to me.

I know what David meant when he wrote these beautiful words.

Surely goodness and mercy shall follow me all the days of my life: and I will dwell in the house of the Lord forever. (Psalm 23:6)

I am sure you wonder what this has to do with this book, and especially what it has to do with Jesus. So, I will explain it to you.

Throughout the pages of this book, I have endeavored to relate to you the many ways in which the life of Jesus affects your life. I have worked diligently to present the human side of Jesus as clearly and accurately as possible. I wrote a book about His relationships to help you understand why this matters. Because if there is anything good about your life, it is because of Him. For that, you should be grateful. When I apply this to my life, I am incredibly grateful.

My real purpose in authoring this book was to help you figure out who you are. Most of all, I wanted to help you figure out who you should be. Then, above all of that, I wanted to help you believe you could be who God wants you to be.

I have done my best in what I have written, never to be disrespectful or to even sound disrespectful of the Lord Jesus.

My Conclusions

There are those who would think I have failed at that because I made so much out of Jesus being a man. I have only tried to describe the Son of man. That is who Jesus said He was. He was a man just like us, who experienced many types of human relationships just like we do.

In case that may still bother some who read this, I will point out one more thing from the verses I have used as a foundation for this book.

> *When Jesus came into the region of Caesarea Philippi, He asked His disciples, saying, "Who do men say that I, the Son of Man, am?" So they said, "Some say John the Baptist, some Elijah, and others Jeremiah or one of the prophets." He said to them, "But who do you say that I am?" Simon Peter answered and said, "You are the Christ, the Son of the living God." (Matthew 16:13-16 – NKJV))*

The question that Jesus asked them was this: *"Who do men say that I, the **Son of Man**, am?"* The question was about the Son of **Man**. In all fairness to the disciples, I will point out that Jesus had focused on the issue of Him being a "man," and those are the types of answers Jesus received. They named John the Baptist, Elijah, and Jeremiah. These were men.

No doubt you have noticed that the answer that Peter gave was very different. In essence, Peter said, "You are the Son of God." Peter's response to who Jesus was as a man was to say that He was the Son of God. They are one and the same.

This is the reason for the response that Jesus gave. Peter was the first to grasp this fact. To declare that Jesus was both the Son of man and the Son of God was not just unusual; **it was unheard of**. This could only come through revelation.

I have saved this information until the conclusion of this book for a simple reason. It is this. When we look deeply enough at every relationship that Jesus had, we can see the evidence that Jesus was both the Son of God and the Son of man. I desire you to see this in all the different situations in His life. My intention was not to confuse you but rather to convince you that this is true. Why do I think this is so important? It matters because of what it says about you.

I must admit that seeing the evidence of this "dual" nature does not mean we fully understand it. Understanding this magnificent aspect of Jesus was, is, and will be a struggle that will not end in this life. Ultimately, it is a matter of faith.

I hope that what I have discussed here and what will come in the next volume will serve to enhance your faith in what we know to be true. Don't be concerned about proving these things. That is both impossible and unnecessary.

Now, my next question may take things too far when some read it, but I do believe it is valid. Do you think Jesus ever wondered about what was in store for Him? Did He ever experience any anxiety? What He did is so astounding it is hard to believe Jesus really approached His life the way we approach ours. Yet, we do have this statement.

My Conclusions

> *For we have not an high priest which cannot be touched with the feeling of our infirmities; but was in all points tempted like as we are, yet without sin. (Hebrews 4:15)*

How far can we take those statements? How far should we take that? I am going to leave those answers up to you. I will only say this. Of all the things I have spoken of in this book, none of it was done for the sole benefit of Jesus. In fact, everything He did, including every relationship He had, including the one with Judas Iscariot, was for our benefit. Those are amazing things to think about.

So, finally, it all comes down to this. You thought you were reading about who Jesus is. You were. But ultimately you have been reading about who God wants you to be. You have been reading about who you can be. You are someone's daughter or someone's son. But if you are a Christian, that means you are also the daughter or the son of God.

You know I don't mean you can die for the sins of the World. Of course, you are not a deity and able to sit at the right hand of the Father and make intercession for the rest of us. You were not here before the World was. You have not yet been raised from the dead like Jesus was. Maybe you don't need me to say those things, but I never know who may read this book.

Statements like those above cause me to think of a passage that means more to me every time I read it.

> *I am crucified with Christ: nevertheless I live; yet not I, but Christ liveth in me: and the life which I now live in the flesh I live by the faith of the Son of God, who loved me, and gave himself for me. (Galatians 2:20)*

That is the best description I have ever read of who we are. *The life I now live in the flesh* so accurately describes our life after we are born again. We are still here on this planet. We still have the same body, but we do not have the same life.

Here is the truth. *I live by the faith of the Son of God, who loved me, and gave himself for me.*

Since I have chosen to fully embrace those words, it is incumbent upon me to know as much as possible about this person called the Son of God. And as strange as it may seem, the best source of that knowledge and revelation is found in what we know about the Son of man.

It was not my idea. I just told you God's idea. That is what you have been reading. But this isn't all. There is more to be said in the Epilogue.

God Bless You!
Dr. Ken Stewart

Epilogue

As I have stated previously, this book is the first of a two-volume set. I did not plan it to be that way. I just found I had gathered far too much material for one book. The tremendous amount of material I discovered about who Jesus was and is must be treated both efficiently and effectively. This required more research and more writing. Ultimately, there must be another book. And I will assure you that there will be.

After finishing the original manuscript, I was surprised and pleased to see how the Holy Spirit had led me. Frankly, I think "thrilled" is a better and more accurate description of my feelings about what the Holy Spirit has allowed me to write.

When I began to follow the direction of the Lord in splitting this information into two volumes, my first reaction was to wonder where I should make the break. I looked at the Contents page of Volume 1, and I saw it immediately. I also understood the reason for this direction from the Holy Ghost.

This first volume is focused on the relationships Jesus had as the Son of man. This begins with His relationship with His Father. Then, we learn things about His relationship with the Holy Spirit. Next is the discussion of Jesus's relationship with His natural family.

From that vantage point, it was a simple transition to writing about "His Friends" and "His Disciples." Of course, the book ends with the strangest of all relationships. That is His relationship with Judas Iscariot. All of this was easy for me to see. It was the next volume of which I was uncertain.

Then, suddenly, I could see very clearly what the Lord had been leading me to do over the past few months. In the next volume, you will find a completely different focus. It is not about relationships.

Think of it this way. If this book is about how Jesus reached out to others and shared His life with them, then in a profound sense, the next volume is about Jesus turning inward. I will put this in the form of some questions to help you understand.

Jesus needed these human relationships. He needed all of them just like we do. He needed to show how He (as a man) related to His Heavenly Father. We needed that.

But what else did Jesus need? What were the most important things that Jesus did that made Him who He was as the Son of God and the Son of man?

Epilogue

Can we not say it was how he prayed and the things the Holy Spirit revealed to Him when He was praying? I believe so. We can have the most wonderful human relationships it is possible to have, but if the truth is never revealed to us, we have nothing of real value to put into those relationships. Perhaps you have never thought of Jesus in this way.

I have kept the same title for Volume 2. Jesus did want to know what the people, and especially His disciples, were saying about who He was. But wasn't it more important for Jesus to know who He was?

What did Jesus think of His gifts? What about His self-esteem, and did He remember the relationship He had with His Father before He became a man?

Jesus was constantly mocked and ridiculed. He was called a fraud, a liar, a false prophet, and was even (in so many words) called the devil. At least they said He was using the power of the devil. So, I have another question. Did Jesus care about His reputation? We sure tend to care about ours.

These are the topics in the next volume. They are all about Jesus, and there are many other topics that I will be exploring that I will not take the space to mention now. Perhaps from this, you can understand what I mean when I say the next book is an inward look at Jesus.

In case you are wondering if this is all found in the Bible, the answer is absolutely yes. I would not be writing it if it wasn't. I can't wait for you to read it so I will publish the next volume as soon as possible. When you have finished both volumes, I have no doubt you will have discovered what I have discovered. I thought I knew Him.

I don't mean I thought I was born-again. I knew that much. That was settled long ago. I did know Jesus in many ways, but now my understanding of Him is much richer. He means more to me than He ever has, and I have known Him for many years as my Lord, my Savior, and my friend. It may not sound just right, but now, I feel like I have walked a few steps in His shoes. Obviously, I am speaking of a closeness that I trust you will experience as well.

You will be able to order "Who Do Men Say That I AM" Volume 2 on Amazon.com.

Notes

[1] 1 John 3:8 (KJ21) He that committeth sin is of the devil, for the devil sinneth from the beginning. For this purpose the Son of God was manifested, that He might destroy the works of the devil.

[2] "G2316 - theos - Strong's Greek Lexicon (kjv)." Blue Letter Bible. Web. 23 Dec, 2023. <https://www.blueletterbible.org/lexicon/g2316/kjv/tr/0-1/>.

[3] "G2316 - theos - Strong's Greek Lexicon (kjv)." Blue Letter Bible. Web. 23 Dec, 2023. <https://www.blueletterbible.org/lexicon/g2316/kjv/tr/0-1/>.

[4] "G2424 - iēsous - Strong's Greek Lexicon (kjv)." Blue Letter Bible. Web. 23 Dec, 2023. <https://www.blueletterbible.org/lexicon/g2424/kjv/tr/0-1/>.

[5] "G40 - hagios - Strong's Greek Lexicon (kjv)." Blue Letter Bible. Web. 23 Dec, 2023. <https://www.blueletterbible.org/lexicon/g40/kjv/tr/0-1/>.

[6] "G4151 - pneuma - Strong's Greek Lexicon (kjv)." Blue Letter Bible. Web. 23 Dec, 2023. <https://www.blueletterbible.org/lexicon/g4151/kjv/tr/0-1/>.

[7] Written by: Ninian Smart   Fact-checked by: The Editors of Encyclopedia Britannica Last Updated: Jan 8, 2025
polytheism is the belief in many gods. Polytheism characterizes virtually all religions other than Judaism, Christianity, and Islam, which share a common tradition of monotheism, the belief in one God.

[8] "H3162 - yaḥad - Strong's Hebrew Lexicon (kjv)." Blue Letter Bible. Web. 16 May, 2024. <https://www.blueletterbible.org/lexicon/h3162/kjv/wlc/0-1/>.

[9] Lyrics are in eminent domain.

[10] I often quote passages from the NIV. When I use this translation of the New International Version, it is always the version that was released on October 27, 1978. There have been other revisions since then. You will discover that there are verses that are missing in the NIV. Most disturbing is the 2011 revision, which is gender-neutral. To me, this is more than absurd. You may wonder why I continue to use quotes from the NIV. I am very careful with what I use from every translation. However, I am always searching for sources that make things clearer without creating doctrinal issues. I am a theologian. I am well-established in what I believe. This should be clear from

my writing. So I want it to be clear that my occasional use of the NIV is in no manner an endorsement of the translation as a whole. I most certainly do not agree with the changes made in the most recent revision.

[11] 1 Corinthians 12: 1-11

[12] There are many translations of the Bible available. It should not be assumed that these translations are equally reliable. Each of them has an inherent theological characteristic. There are two major types of translations. The first one is the Textus Receptus. Textus Receptus (received texts) is the name given to a series of Greek texts of the New Testament which were printed between 1500 and 1900. The name Textus Receptus was first used to refer to editions of the Greek New Testament published in 1633. The name has been retrospectively applied to all the printed Greek texts of the same text-type. Textus Receptus was established on the Majority Text, which represents over 90% of the 5,800+ Greek manuscripts of the New Testament still in existence today. Textus Receptus contains the translation base for the first Greek translation of the New Testament into English by William Tyndale, and it is the textual base for the King James Bible and, therefore, the New King James Bible.

The other major translations are based on the Nestle-Aland Greek New Testament (N) and the United Bible Society's third edition (U). When you look at different translations and you see a footnote that refers to (NU) this is a reference to something that is based on one or both of these Greek New Testaments. The Nestle-Aland Greek New Testament and the United Bible Society's Greek New Testament are said to be identical. This type of translation is committed to presenting variations of the text based on the oldest text available, such as the Alexandrian or Egyptian type of text. A major problem (in my opinion) is that some of the oldest texts are also some of the most questionable and unreliable texts that we have. As an astute student of the Bible you will notice these issues even if you have never studied the Biblical languages.

At times I have included quotes from the ESV, the NIV and perhaps other newer translations. I check these very carefully before I use them. I want to be sure the verses I quote do not include doctrinal issues with which I disagree. I use these translations because some of them are easier to understand than the old King James Version. My intention in presenting this information in these notes is not to paint these newer translations with a broad brush of complete disapproval. Rather, I have inserted this disclaimer as a simple but sincere word of caution.

All of the translations I know anything about can be tied back to one of the two original sources I have mentioned. The older ones are based on the Textus Receptus or some effort at an update. The modern translations are based on the Nestle-Aland

Greek New Testament and the United Bible Society's Greek New Testament. It is more than a matter of when they were translated. It is what is behind the translation — the bias is what matters.

[13] See End Note 12.

[14] "G1849 - exousia - Strong's Greek Lexicon (kjv)." Blue Letter Bible. Web. 13 May, 2024. <https://www.blueletterbible.org/lexicon/g1849/kjv/tr/0-1/>.

[15] "G5319 - phaneroō - Strong's Greek Lexicon (kjv)." Blue Letter Bible. Web. 5 Jan, 2025. <https://www.blueletterbible.org/lexicon/g5319/kjv/tr/0-1/>.

[16] "G4624 - skandalizō - Strong's Greek Lexicon (kjv)." Blue Letter Bible. Web. 23 Dec, 2023. <https://www.blueletterbible.org/lexicon/g4624/kjv/tr/0-1/>.

[17] "G570 - apistia - Strong's Greek Lexicon (kjv)." Blue Letter Bible. Web. 23 Dec, 2023. <https://www.blueletterbible.org/lexicon/g570/kjv/tr/0-1/>.

[18] "G211 - alabastron - Strong's Greek Lexicon (kjv)." Blue Letter Bible. Web. 15 Jan, 2024. <https://www.blueletterbible.org/lexicon/g211/kjv/tr/0-1/>.

[19] "G3464 - myron - Strong's Greek Lexicon (kjv)." Blue Letter Bible. Web. 15 Jan, 2024. <https://www.blueletterbible.org/lexicon/g3464/kjv/tr/0-1/>.

[20] Britannica, The Editors of Encyclopedia. "St. Thomas". Encyclopedia Britannica, 11 Apr. 2024, https://www.britannica.com/biography/Saint-Thomas. Accessed 31 May 2024.

[21] See End Note 10.

[22] Jamieson, R., Fausset, A. R., & Brown, D. (1997). "*Commentary Critical and Explanatory on the Whole Bible*" (Vol. 2). Oak Harbor, WA: Logos Research Systems, Inc., 129.

And two of his disciples. —One was Andrew, we know from ver. 40 (see Com. on Matthew ch. 10:1–4); the other was certainly John. We judge thus from (1) John's manner of mentioning himself, either not at all, or indirectly (chs. 13:23; 18:15; 19:26; 20:3; 21:20); a manner which he seems to have extended also to his mother (19:25; comp. Introduction, p. 5), and to which we might cite analogies in Mark (ch. 14:51) and Luke (ch. 24:18). 2) The giving of one name, suggesting a personal reserve in regard to the other. 3) The very lifelike character of the subsequent account. 4) The more distinct calling of the sons of Zebedee immediately after, with the sons of Jonas, on the sea of Galilee, Matth. 4. As the calling of the latter is introduced here, so is doubtless the calling of the former.

[23] "G2199 - zebedaios - Strong's Greek Lexicon (kjv)." Blue Letter Bible. Web. 18 Jan, 2024. <https://www.blueletterbible.org/lexicon/g2199/kjv/tr/0-1/>.

[24] "G993 - boanērges - Strong's Greek Lexicon (kjv)." Blue Letter Bible. Web. 19 Jan, 2024. <https://www.blueletterbible.org/lexicon/g993/kjv/tr/0-1/>.

[25] 1 Corinthians 12:8 (KJV) For to one is given by the Spirit the word of wisdom; to another the word of knowledge by the same Spirit;

[26] 1 Corinthians 12:1-11

[27] 1 Corinthians 12:8

[28] 1 Corinthians 12:10 (KJV) To another the working of miracles; to another prophecy; to another discerning of spirits; to another divers kinds of tongues; to another the interpretation of tongues:

[29] Most material © 2005, 1997, 1991 by Penguin Random House LLC. Modified entries © 2019 by Penguin Random House LLC and HarperCollins Publishers Ltd.

[30] "G1253 - diakrisis - Strong's Greek Lexicon (kjv)." Blue Letter Bible. Web. 18 Jan, 2024. <https://www.blueletterbible.org/lexicon/g1253/kjv/tr/0-1/>.

[31] This was "truth" this man had not known previously. It was "truth" he would never have known without the aid of the Holy Spirit.

[32] 1 Corinthians 12:8 (KJV) For to one is given by the Spirit the word of wisdom; to another the word of knowledge by the same Spirit;

[33] 1 Corinthians 12:10 (KJV) To another the working of miracles; to another prophecy; to another discerning of spirits; to another divers kinds of tongues; to another the interpretation of tongues:

[34] Acts 2:14 (KJV) But Peter, standing up with the eleven, lifted up his voice, and said unto them, Ye men of Judaea, and all ye that dwell at Jerusalem, be this known unto you, and hearken to my words:

³⁵ Luke 2:13-14 (KJV) And suddenly there was with the angel a multitude of the heavenly host praising God, and saying, Glory to God in the highest, and on earth peace, good will toward men.

³⁶ "G2581 - kananaios - Strong's Greek Lexicon (kjv)." Blue Letter Bible. Web. 19 Jan, 2024. <https://www.blueletterbible.org/lexicon/g2581/kjv/tr/0-1/>.

³⁷ "G3002 - lebbaios - Strong's Greek Lexicon (kjv)." Blue Letter Bible. Web. 18 Jan, 2024. <https://www.blueletterbible.org/lexicon/g3002/kjv/tr/0-1/>.

³⁸ "G2280 - thaddaios - Strong's Greek Lexicon (kjv)." Blue Letter Bible. Web. 18 Jan, 2024. <https://www.blueletterbible.org/lexicon/g2280/kjv/tr/0-1/>.

³⁹ "G3338 - metamelomai - Strong's Greek Lexicon (kjv)." Blue Letter Bible. Web. 10 Jan, 2025. <https://www.blueletterbible.org/lexicon/g3338/kjv/tr/0-1/>.
The old King James Bible has this translated as "Then Judas, which had betrayed him, when he saw that he was condemned, repented himself." The NIV says "remorse".

About the Author

Dr Ken Stewart is a prominent figure in the Christian community, with over 60 years of experience in ministry and education. He is a respected author, pastor, and educator whose teachings have impacted countless individuals and families across the United States and beyond.

Born and raised in Arkansas, Dr Stewart had an early calling to ministry. When he was just a child, Dr. Stewart would set up his idea of a church service on his front porch and preach to the neighborhood kids. It may have looked to the adults like he was playing, but it was serious business to him.

After receiving his Bachelor of Science Degree from Southwestern Assemblies of God College, Dr. Stewart attended Brite Divinity School at Texas Christian University in Fort Worth, Texas, where he received his Master of Divinity degree. He completed his Doctor of Ministry degree from the same institution, solidifying his knowledge and passion for serving the Lord.

Dr Stewart began his adult ministry as a pastor, serving several churches in Texas and Oklahoma. He quickly gained a reputation for his straightforward and easy-to-understand teaching style, which drew people from all walks of life to his congregations.

Over time, Dr Stewart's ministry expanded beyond the church walls. He became a sought-after speaker, traveling across the United States and abroad to share his knowledge and experience with others. Dr. Stewart has spoken in over 2000 different churches and in 19 different denominations. This speaks very highly of the level of acceptance his ministry has received over the past 60 years. He has spoken at countless conferences, retreats, and seminars, inspiring and educating audiences of all ages and backgrounds.

In addition to his work as a pastor and speaker, Dr Stewart is also an accomplished author. He has written 18 books covering various topics related to the Christian faith. His writing is engaging, thought-provoking, and inspiring, and he has helped countless individuals and families grow in their faith.

One of Dr Stewart's most recent books, "The New Covenant Psalm: Psalm 91 in the Light of the New Testament," offers a fresh perspective on one of the Bible's most beloved Psalms. The Psalm focuses on dealing with fear. Dr Stewart provides practical insights on trusting God for protection and safety in a world filled with violence and danger. The book has been well-received by readers and has helped many find peace and security in their daily lives.

Dr Stewart's ministry has also focused on family relationships. He understands that financial difficulties cause many marital problems. To help couples navigate these challenges, he enrolled in the Graduate Business Center of Florida Tech in St. Petersburg, Florida, to study Financial Planning. He completed his training at Northeastern State University in Broken Arrow, OK. Having gained this knowledge, Dr Stewart acquired the necessary licenses and started his own business, spanning 18 states and managing retirement plans for approximately 400 clients.

Dr Stewart's extensive experience in ministry, education, and financial planning has made him a trusted advisor and mentor to many. His teachings are grounded in the Word of God and reflect his deep understanding of the human experience. His writing is accessible and inspiring. His insights into faith and Christian living have helped countless individuals and families find hope, healing, and peace.

In all his work, Dr Stewart remains committed to serving the Lord and sharing His message of love, grace, and redemption with the world. He continues to write, speak, and mentor, inspiring and encouraging others to grow in their faith and deepen their relationship with God.

*Empowering Believers
to do the Works of Jesus!*

Online Classes
shs.drkenstewart.com
Mailing Address: PO Box 470492 Tulsa, OK 74147

P O Box 470492
Tulsa, OK 74147

www.ingramcontent.com/pod-product-compliance
Lightning Source LLC
Chambersburg PA
CBHW060508090426
42735CB00011B/2143